Reproducible

ART ACTIVITIES
WITH PAPER, CLAY, FIBERS, AND PRINTMAKING
Using Masterworks as Inspiration

Consultant:
Kay Alexander

CrystalProductions
Glenview, IL

Art Activities with Paper, Clay, Fibers, and Printmaking: Using Masterworks as Inspiration

CUTTING, TEARING, FOLDING, AND FASTENING ACTIVITIES

Grade/Pages	Activity	Concept	Skill	Resource	Description
K–1 6-7	Balancing Act	Symmetry and asymmetry	Organizing and pasting	**Student Work**	Geometric shapes are arranged to create symmetrical or asymmetrical designs, then pasted down.
K–1 8-9	Holey Cylinders	Art projects using scrap paper	Piercing and tearing openings in paper	**Student Work**	Holes are torn in paper, which is then wrapped around a solid piece of paper to form a cylinder.
1–3 10-11	Tissue and Foil Collage	Overlapping translucent papers creates new colors	Overlapping tissue shapes and gluing	**Student Work**	Torn pieces of tissue paper are glued to aluminum foil to make flexible, luminous paper.
2–3 12-13	Fan-Fold Forms	Many forms can be made with fan-folded paper	Accurate fan-folding and fastening	**Flowers and Birds Chinese Fan** Chiang Ting-Shi	Children learn to fan-fold, then use the fans to build paper sculptures.
2–3 14-15	Torn Paper Landscapes	A landscape is a collection of individual features	Controlled tearing of construction paper and magazine pages	**Canyon** Ki Davis	After identifying features found in a landscape, students tear and combine colored paper pieces to make a landscape collage.
2–3 16-17	Shapes and Textures	Collage is a technique in which materials are fastened to a backing	Organizing shapes of various textures into a composition	**Guitar** Georges Braques	Materials with different textures are selected, cut, and arranged on a backing to make a collage.
2–3 18-19	Texture Towers	Slotted cards can be fitted together to make a sculpture	Fastening shapes without using glue or tape	**House of Cards** Charles Eames	Textured materials are cut and glued to precut slotted cards and then assembled into a sculptural form.
4–6 20-21	Slot Sculpture	Flat shapes can be connected by notching	Building forms from flat planes without glue	**Nessie** Rita Blitt	Pieces of cardboard are cut out to resemble an animal. Slots are cut into the pieces to join them, then the pieces are painted.
4–6 22-23	Lines Create Shapes	A line is the edge of a shape	Cutting and gluing	**Composition, Black and Red** Henri Matisse	Cut a continuous, meandering, noncrossing line through a sheet of paper. Separate the parts and glue to a contrasting paper.
4–6 24-25	Illusion of Form	Shading produces the illusion of volume	Learning to shade cylinders and spheres	**The Basket of Apples** Paul Cézanne	Students cut shapes of different kinds of fruit and vegetables and color them with oil pastels. The pieces are arranged and glued to a background paper to make a still life.
5–6 26-27	Haiku Book	Art can be functional	Measuring, folding, cutting, gluing	**Japanese Haiku Books**	Students make an accordion book with dip-dyed paper covers tied with ribbon.
4–8 28-29	Scribbles and Nibbles: Tear Into Action	The human figure in action is a subject of artists	Tearing and fastening	**Snap the Whip** Winslow Homer	Make gesture figure drawings, tear them out, and glue them to colored paper.
6–8 30-31	Paper-Cut Designs	Many cultures create folk art with cut paper	Precise cutting, folding, and fastening	**Wycinanki** Czeslawa Konopka	Fold and cut a paper design like the Polish folk cut-outs and then glue them to a colored background paper.

Activities Overview

FIBERS AND DESIGNING ACTIVITIES

Grade/ Pages	Activity	Concept	Skill	Resource	Description
K–1 32-33	Cardboard Weaving	A woven fabric consists of warp and weft.	Learning basic tabby weaving.	*Landscape* Carolyn Hedstrom	Through a string or yarn warp on notched cardboard, children weave yarn, fabric strips, raffia, and paper.
2–3 34-35	Yarn Paintings	Colored yarn "lines" can make shapes and designs.	Simulating a Mexican craft.	*Huichol Yarn Painting*	White glue can be used to adhere yarn to cardboard to simulate Huichol yarn paintings.
2–3 36-37	Paper Mask	Masks are symmetrical designs derived from facial features.	Designing a mask with paper.	*North American Native American Mask*	Geometric shapes are drawn with chalk on paper and exaggerated features are added to the shapes to make a mask.
2–3 38-39	Banners	Banners incorporate graphics, symbols, and borders to give a message.	Designing a personal banner.	*Art Museum Banners*	A banner is made with paper, and cut-out letters and symbols are glued to the banner.
3–4 40-41	Adinkra Prints	Printing can be used to decorate textiles.	Relief printing on fabric.	*Adinkra Cloth, Ghana*	A simple design becomes a blockprint pattern to decorate fabric in the West African manner.
3–4 42-43	Paper Molas	People use design to decorate their clothing.	Simulating a Panamanian craft with cut paper.	*Cuna Indian Mola*	Students simulate a mola with colored paper shapes glued in layers representing an animal or bird.
4–6 44-45	Name Patterns	Letter shapes can be used as design elements.	Creating a pattern by using letter shapes.	*Once Emerged from the Gray of Night #3* Paul Klee	Students print their names in a grid with one letter to a square, then paint the negative spaces around the letters to create a pattern.
4–6 46-47	Quilt Blocks	Geometric shapes can be repeated to form patterns and enhance functional objects.	Arranging geometric shapes to form patterns.	*Fanfare* Molly Upton	Using only squares and triangles and limited colors, students will explore and establish individual patterns.
4–6 48-49	Crayon Batik	Batik is a design process originating in Southeast Asia used for coloring textiles.	Simulating the batik process with crayons.	*Indonesian Batik*	Colored crayons and paraffin are melted and painted on a cloth. The cloth is dyed and the wax melted with an iron to create a batik.
5–6 50-51	Weaving in the Round	Weaving can be a kind of sculpture.	Making a tapestry "in the round."	*The Hand* Magdalena Abakanowicz	Using a notched cardboard cylinder as a loom, students warp it and weave yarns around it to create a dimensional weaving.
5–8 52-53	Big Bold Banners	Banners and hangings are decorative devices.	Designing and making a fabric banner.	*Student Work*	Students design and craft personal banners of felt, gluing on cut-out symbols and enhancing them with yarn.
6–8 54-55	Words That Do What They Say	"The medium is the message."	Applied design.	*Road Sign*	Create from various materials letters that form words that describe what they say.
6–8 56-57	Coiled Baskets	A container can be made from coiled, wrapped fiber.	Learning the coil technique of basketry.	*Navajo Basket*	Yarn is wrapped around a length of jute. The just and yarn are coiled to make a basket.

Modeling and Constructing Activities

Grade/Pages	Activity	Concept	Skill	Resource	Description
K–3 58-59	**Clay Owl Ornament**	Clay is malleable	Imprinting and folding a clay slab	**Owl** Pablo Picasso	An oval slab of clay is shaped into an owl form and then textured with found objects
K–3 60-61	**Clay Hang Ups**	Impressing objects in clay creates textures. Clay forms can make a mobile	Imprinting clay to make a texture surface and joining with pieces of string	**Beebop** Timothy Rose	Clay slabs are cut into different shapes, textured, and joined with string to make a mobile
1–3 62-63	**Fancy Strips**	Paper can be manipulated into three-dimensional forms	Combining curled and folded strips	**Student Work**	Students make a shallow box and fill it with folded and curled strips of multicolored paper
2–3 64-65	**Birds, Butterflies, and Flowers**	Two-dimensional paper can make three-dimensional forms	Constructing forms from manipulated paper strips	**Student Work**	Curling and folding colored paper into birds, butterflies, flowers, and symmetrical designs
2–3 66-67	**Dragon Puppet**	A puppet can be made from a sock	Designing and making a hand puppet	**Student Work**	A tube sock is decorated with felt, feathers, and pipe cleaners to become a dragon hand puppet
2–3 68-69	**Cylinder Sillies**	Paper can be formed and decorated	Cutting, folding, fringing, piercing, and fastening	**Women and Dog** Marisol	Simple paper sculpture techniques are applied to a cylinder to make clown-like faces
2–3 70-71	**Helmet Mask**	Some masks are worn over the top of the head, like a helmet	Constructing a cardboard-strip helmet and decorating it	**African Bamun and Bakuba Helmet Masks**	Cardboard strips are fastened into a helmet which is decorated with paper hair, eyes, ears, nose, and mouth
4–5 72-73	**Cutting a Figure**	The parts of the human figure are in relative proportion	Representing the figure by assembling parts into a whole	**Both Members of this Club** George Bellows	A head, body, arms, and legs are drawn and cut from heavy paper, then fastened together to make a two-dimensional mannequin
4–6 74-75	**Slab Animals**	Clay can be rolled, cut, textured, and formed	Rolling slabs, cutting, decorating, and forming clay shapes	**Student Work**	A "bear rug" symmetrical animal is cut from a clay slab, textured, formed, and dried. It can be painted or fired and glazed.
5–6 76-77	**Origami Boxes**	Useful objects may be formed from paper	Accurate folding and forming of paper	**Student Work**	Two squares of paper are folded into a box and cover, then decorated, if desired
5–6 78-79	**Mosaic Mask**	Masks can be formed over the face and decorated with a paper mosaic	Modeling foil and creating a paper mosaic	**Aztec Mask**	A foil mask is folded on the face and painted black, then decorated with colorad paper mosaic pieces cut from magazine pages
5–8 80-81	**Piñata Party**	A Mexican vessel that is meant to be destroyed	Compound forms combined and decorated	**Mexican Piñata**	Cardboard forms are fastened together and decorated with tissue paper to make a piñata
5–8 82-83	**Model: Interior of a Room**	Interior designers develop floor plans and wall elevations	Making a cardboard cube and drawing a floor plan and elevations of a room	**Interior Model of a Building** Harry Teague	A cardboard cube is made and the floor plan and elevations of a room are drawn and painted on the interior surfaces
5–8 84-85	**Portrait on a Pole**	Sculptors work with armatures	Modeling a clay head on an armature	**Alexandre Brongniart** Jean-Antoine Houdon	A dowel on a board is covered with a paper bag filled with newspaper and used as an armature. Clay slabs are added and a head is sculpted

Activities Overview

PRINTMAKING ACTIVITIES

Grade/Pages	Activity	Concept	Skill	Resource	Description
K–2 86-87	Clay and Gadget Prints	More than one print can be made from a printing plate	Creating a stamp design in clay and printing it	**Cylinder Seal**	A plasticene relief stamp is used to make multiple prints. Found objects are inked and printed on paper
1–3 88-89	Fingerpaint Monoprints	A monoprint is a one-of-a-kind print	Planographic monoprinting with finger paint	**Anne's Roses** Sandra Kaplan	A monoprint is made by two children. One makes a fingerpainting and the other lays a piece of paper over the fingerpainting to make a monoprint
1–3 90-91	Chalk Stencils	Stencil as a "block out" technique	Preparing a stencil and printing from it	**Comedy** Kannak	A pueblo-shaped stencil is cut out of cardboard, and chalk is rubbed on the edge which is brushed onto the printing paper several times
2–3 92-93	Nature Prints	Structure and texture of natural objects may be printed	Use of a brayer	**Student Work**	Leaves are collected, pressed, inked, and printed on different colored papers and painted backgrounds
2–3 94-95	Exploded Designs	A relief block can be made from cardboard	Making a built-up cardboard relief block and printing it	**White is the Best Color** Glen Alps	Cutting cardboard pieces, expanding and arranging them on a larger cardboard which is sealed, inked, and printed
2–3 96-97	Glue and String Prints	Glue and glued string create linear designs that can be printed	Creating a linear collagraph and printing from it	**Student Work**	Glue is traced along a linear drawing to create a relief printing plate. Glue and string are also used in the same way to make collagraphs
3–4 98-99	Multicolor Cardboard Printing	Cardboard relief prints can be multicolored	Printing in register	**Mt. Fuji in Clear Weather** Katsushika Hokusai	A cardboard relief plate is printed in white. The plate and paper are registered and additional colors are printed
4–6 100-101	Japanese Paint Prints	A paint print can simulate a Japanese woodblock print	Designing and printing a simulated woodblock print	**Horse Mackerel and Prawn** Ando Hiroshige	Paper is taped to the end of a styrofoam plate which is painted with watercolor, one section at a time, and printed
4–6 102-103	Chalk Monoprints	Monoprinting may be combined with chalk for a mixed media print	Combining chalk drawing with monoprinting	**Einstein on the Beach III** Red Grooms	A design is filled in with chalk, placed face down on an inked styropad and the lines redrawn. The chalk is fixed by the printing ink and the lines will appear dark
4–6 104-105	Textured Collagraphs	Textured prints can be made from textural collages	Making a collagraph from a textural collage	**Growing Hill** Glen Alps	Different materials with different textures are cut and arranged into a collage which is inked and printed
5–6 106-107	Acetate Intaglio	An intaglio print is made by transferring the ink in the scratches of a plate to paper	Making a drypoint intaglio print	**Self Portrait** Rembrandt van Rijn	A clear plastic sheet is placed over a drawing and the image scratched into the plastic which is then inked, wiped, and printed
5–8 108-109	Corrugated Collagraphs	A corrugated relief print uses textures to create light, middle, and dark values	Creating a print in three values	**The White Square** Glen Alps	A piece of corrugated cardboard is cut to make three textures which when printed will make three different values in the print
6–8 110-111	Linoleum Prints	Linoleum is used by graphic artists to make relief prints	Applied design	**Still Life Under a Lamp** Pablo Picasso	A design is drawn on a linoleum block which is cut, inked, and printed

Art Activities with Paper, Clay, Fibers, and Printmaking: Using Masterworks as Inspiration

1 Balancing Act

Grade Level
K–1

Concept
Symmetry and asymmetry — formal and informal balance.

Skill
Organizing and pasting.

Resource
Student works.

Materials
Assorted precut shapes of a variety of colored papers, about 1 x 2 inches in shallow containers for each group of children; black or white paper 6 x 9 inches, two pieces per child; glue or paste; toothpicks; scrap paper for glue.

Procedure
Show the examples and discuss their similarities and differences, explaining specifically the symmetry and asymmetry of the paintings. Arrange objects symmetrically on either side of a center, such as a clock and two candlesticks on a mantel. Compare it to the balance of a see-saw: "What must be done when a heavy child sits on one side?" Next, group several objects informally or asymmetrically.

When the children indicate understanding, distribute containers of paper shapes and one piece of 6 x 9-inch paper to the students. Have them fold the paper to find the center and arrange the pieces to make a design with symmetrical (formal) balance. When this has been accomplished and checked, they will lift, one piece at a time, dot it with glue or paste with a toothpick, and fasten it down. On the second piece of 6 x 9-inch paper, students will arrange then fasten down a design showing asymmetrical (informal) balance.

Display the results in pairs and evaluate them using the new vocabulary.

First, we will look at symmetry, or formal balance, and asymmetry, or informal balance. The image on the left is an example of symmetrical balance — the design is balanced evenly on both sides of the collage. The picture on the right is an example of asymmetrical balance — the shapes in the composition are balanced informally.

1 Select different **geometric shapes** and colors cut from construction paper to use in this experience. Can you identify the rectangles, squares, and triangles?

2 First, you will make a symmetrical or formally balanced design. Select two pieces of the same shape and color and place them on either side of the center of a large piece of colored paper.

geometric shapes: shapes that are precise and regular, i.e. squares, circles, triangles, rectangles, etc.

Cutting, Tearing, Folding, and Fastening Activities

3 Select other shapes and place them on the paper. A single shape can be placed directly on the center.

4 Are the shapes and colors placed in a formal balance here? Think about the balance of a seesaw and what must be done when you sit on one side and no one is on the other. It must be balanced with someone of equal weight.

5 When you have determined that you have a symmetrical, or evenly balanced, composition, you can glue each shape down on the paper. Composition is the way you arrange your subject.

6 This is the finished piece showing a *symmetrical* composition.

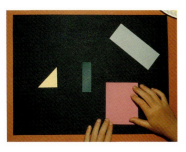

7 Now, explore making an *asymmetrical*, or informally balanced, composition. Place other colored shapes on another piece of paper.

8 Continue adding colored shapes informally until you have a pleasing composition. Then, glue the pieces down.

9 This is a completed asymmetrical composition.

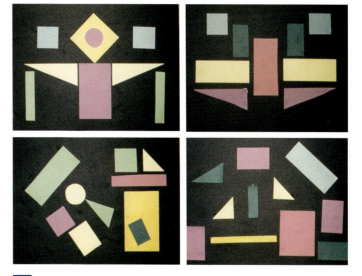

10 Here are four pictures that show symmetrical and asymmetrical compositions. Can you identify them? You are correct if you said the symmetrical or formally balanced compositions were on top, and the asymmetrical or informally balanced compositions were on the bottom.

7

Art Activities with Paper, Clay, Fibers, and Printmaking: Using Masterworks as Inspiration

2 Holey Cylinders

Grade Level
4-6

Concept
Two art projects use every scrap of paper.

Skill
Piercing and tearing openings in paper.

Resource
Student work

Materials
Three pieces of 9 x 12-inch or 12 x 18-inch construction paper of contrasting colors; paste or glue.

Procedure
Show the example and analyze how the "spots" on the mat have been torn from the paper that has been formed into a cylinder. Demonstrate how to pinch a piece of paper and tear the pinch to start a hole. Repeat, making several holes of different sizes and saving the scraps.

Children will tear 7-9 holes, small and larger, in one piece of paper. Next, they will lay the "holey" piece on a contrasting paper, roll it into a cylinder, and fasten the overlapping edges with glue, tape, or staples. (The two pieces of paper can be spot-glued to hold them in place while making a cylinder.) Then, students will glue or paste the scraps onto the third paper to make a pleasing-to-them abstract design. This may be used as a placemat, a folder cover, or the start of a drawing of an imaginary spotted animal.

The cylinders may be hung in the window or encase a milk carton that holds flowers or a dried arrangement.

This is a cylinder made from two pieces of paper. The top piece has holes of different shapes torn out of it. After it has been placed over another color of paper, the two have been rolled and fastened into a cylinder. In front of it is a placemat made by gluing the scraps from the holes in the cylinder in an abstract design. **Abstract art** emphasizes design through the composition of shapes and colors.

1 Here are three pieces of paper, two of the same color. You will use these to make your "holey" cylinder.

abstract art: art which uses simplified forms; subject matter may be recognizable or may be completely transformed into shapes, colors, and/or lines

Cutting, Tearing, Folding, and Fastening Activities

2 To begin this activity, you will tear seven to nine holes in one piece of paper. To do this easily, first pinch the paper, then tear the pinch to start a hole.

3 See the different holes this student has torn? They are all a different shape and size. Remember to save your scraps.

4 After you've torn all your holes, glue the "holey" paper onto another piece of paper of a contrasting color.

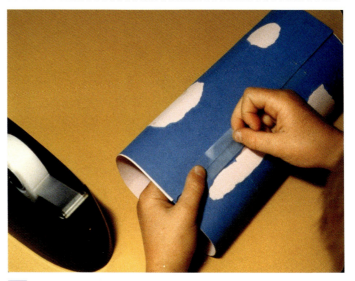

5 Roll the papers into a cylinder, keeping the "holey" side on top and fasten it with tape.

6 Glue the scraps that came from your holes to a colored paper in an interesting design. It can be an abstract design with the scraps placed asymmetrically on the paper. This piece of paper will be the placemat.

7 Here is a completed cylinder holding dried flowers on top of the decorated placemat.

Art Activities with Paper, Clay, Fibers, and Printmaking: Using Masterworks as Inspiration

3 Tissue & Foil Collage

Grade Level
5-6

Concept
Overlapping translucent colored papers creates new colors and values.

Skill
Basic collage techniques.

Resource
Student work

Materials
Heavy-duty aluminum foil; array of colored tissue paper; clear, glossy acrylic polymer; ½- or ¾-inch flat brushes (tempera paint brushes); shallow containers for the polymer; newspapers to cover working area.

Procedure
Overlap pairs of colors of tissue against the light and observe the new colors and values they create. Lay them against white paper or foil and establish the fact that a darker color can be seen through a lighter one but not vice-versa. Therefore, to obtain a new, blended color, the lighter color should be collaged on top of the darker tissues.

Children will tear large, medium, and small shapes from several colors of tissue paper. (All warm or all cool combinations make interesting variations of this lesson.) Children dip the brush into the polymer and paint an area on the foil approximately the size of one of the darker pieces. With the brush, pick up and place the paper on the spot and brush it down with more polymer. Some colors may bleed a bit; ignore it or enjoy it. Polymer can be applied to the paper directly, but it is more difficult. More polymer is brushed on the foil and a lighter-colored tissue overlapped. Observe the effect. Children continue to collage sizes, shapes, and colors to the foil until all of the aluminum is covered. Set aside to dry; then they can trim the edges. The flexible, luminous results can be mounted for display or used for gift wrap or sculpture.

Note: An introductory lesson may be done with white paper, colored tissue, and liquid laundry starch instead of polymer. However, results will not be flexible, like foil collages.

Collage is a technique in which the artist glues materials such as paper, cloth, or found objects onto another material. The collage you see here was made by placing different shapes and colors of tissue paper on a sheet of aluminum foil. The overlapping shapes create new colors and values. Values are the lightness and darkness of a color.

1 Here, you can see how the overlapping part of the blue and yellow tissues, which are **primary colors**, make green, which is a **secondary color**. Be sure to place the lighter color over the darker color to obtain the new, blended color. It will not work as well the reversed way. Try it and see.

primary colors: three main colors (red, yellow, blue) that can be combined to make all other colors

Cutting, Tearing, Folding, and Fastening Activities

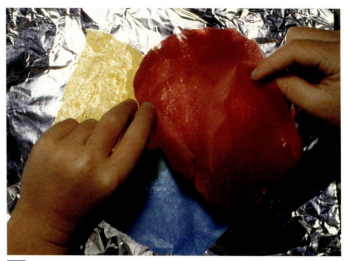

2 Spread out a piece of aluminum foil the size you want your finished work to be. Then, begin carefully tearing out different shapes and colors of tissue paper.

3 Brush polymer emulsion on the foil or on the tissue paper.

4 Then, place the tissue pieces on top of the foil.

5 Continue to add the torn tissue shapes to the foil.

6 Overlap lighter-colored tissue over dark tissue. Observe the effect. Continue to collage sizes, shapes, and colors to the foil.

7 Leave some of the foil uncovered for a sparkling effect to your collage.

8 Some of your shapes may extend off the edge of the foil. These can be trimmed carefully with scissors.

secondary colors: *colors that contain equal amounts of the two primary colors adjacent to them on the color wheel*

9 Here is a completed collage mounted on a mat so that it can be hung on a wall. See if you can find where the overlapping blue and red tissue shapes have made a purple shape.

11

Art Activities with Paper, Clay, Fibers, and Printmaking: Using Masterworks as Inspiration

4 Fan-Fold Forms

Grade Level
6-8

Concept
Many forms can be made with fan-folded paper.

Skill
Accordion folding; choosing appropriate means of fastening.

Resource
Chinese fan with painted flowers and birds by Jiang Tingxi

Materials
9 x 12-inch colored papers; tape, string, glue, and staplers; scissors.

Procedure
Look at the fan-folded part of the fan and explain how a fan opens and closes because of the folding. Brainstorm other uses of the fan-fold. Consider examples of fan-folding in everyday objects: camera bellows, file folders, pleated skirts, etc.

Students will fold a piece of paper in half: place one edge against the opposite edge, matching corners and hold with one hand while pressing with the other. Some creasing will need to be done with a fingernail, scissors handle, or tongue blade. Some will need to be reversed and creased to make a flexible, two-way fold. Fold in half again the same way, and then a third time. Increasing folds will be more difficult. It will be easier to open out the paper and bring the line of one fold up to the next and crease between them, if more than eight divisions are needed. Open and refold each line to make a zigzag.

Have the students experiment with the fan. Pinch it at one end; in the middle; hold in the middle and bring the two ends together, etc. What does each form suggest? Cut, roll, curl, and fasten paper to make a sculpture that uses the fan-fold: a bird, an angel, a butterfly. Fasten the parts together with whichever method works best and shows least.

Small Birds and Morning Glories, early 18th century, Jiang Tingxi, (Chinese, 1669-1732). Qing dynasty. Ink and color on paper, H: 18.5 W: 50.0 cm, China. Transfer from the United States Customs Service, Department of the Treasury F80.152 F1980.152

This is a more than 200-year-old Chinese fan with flowers and birds painted on it. The folded paper has been attached to pieces of wood. It can be closed when not in use, but reveals the beautiful painting when it is opened.

1 We will now explore **accordion-folding** or fan-folding paper to make paper sculptures. Start by folding a piece of paper in half. Then, fold the folded paper in half again. Fold that folded paper in half again. Be sure to make sharp creases by running your fingers firmly over the fold. Open the folded paper and refold each line to make a zigzag, one fold up and the next fold down.

accordion fold: zigzag fold in which a sheet of paper has two or more parallel folds that open in the manner of an accordion.

Cutting, Tearing, Folding, and Fastening Activities

2 Cut out a bird shape from another piece of paper and make a slit in the body of it. Grasp your fan-folded paper in the center and insert it into the bird's body, and you have wings. On the right is a finished bird with fan-folded wings. It looks as though it is flying.

3 To make your next fan-folded form, take a piece of colored paper and fold it in half. Then, fold the folded paper again. Fold that folded paper once more. With the paper still folded, cut a point at each end.

4 After you have refolded the folds to make the zigzag fold, try holding the fan-folded paper in different places. Hold it at the end, then hold it in the middle. The fan will be used both ways in this activity.

5 Three sections of an egg carton will be used to make the body of a flying insect. Paint the egg carton a bright color. After the paint has dried, paint brightly colored spots all over it.

6 Grasp your fan-folded paper in the center and insert it between two of the egg sections. Now, bend two colored pipe cleaners into the shape of a flying insect's antenna and press the wires into the head of the insect. Shape two more colored pipe cleaners for the tail of the insect and insert them into the last egg section.

7 This is a completed flying insect. What does it look like to you? Notice that the student who made this form also painted a face on the head to make his artwork more interesting.

8 Another student made an angel. Two different colors of paper have been glued together. In this case, points were not cut out of the ends. The angel dress has been pinched at one end to fit into the middle of the angel's wings and glued. The student cut a head and is gluing it above the wings.

13

Art Activities with Paper, Clay, Fibers, and Printmaking: Using Masterworks as Inspiration

5 Torn Paper Landscapes

Grade Level
6-8

Concept
A landscape is an arrangement of individual features of forms seen out-of-doors.

Skill
Careful, controlled tearing of construction and craft paper and magazine pages.

Resource
Canyon by Ki Davis

Materials
9 x 12-inch or 12 x 18-inch manila or construction paper; scraps of many colors of paper; old magazines; paste or glue; toothpicks.

Procedure
Analyze the landscape examples for common elements, e.g., trees, roads, buildings, landforms, sky, water. Help students formulate a definition of the term.

Students will tear pieces of paper and assemble them on the support paper to arrange the elements they have identified. Several arrangements should be tried before the glue or paste is distributed. Then, one piece at a time is lifted, touched with glue, and replaced in the composition.

Display the pictures briefly and allow additional worktime so that students may amplify or elaborate their landscape compositions.

Ki Davis, American. *Canyon.* Private collection.

This is a **landscape** collage, an arrangement of individual features or forms that can be seen out-of-doors and which were made from torn paper. This landscape collage was made by American artist Ki Davis who loved nature. Her shapes are abstract, but perhaps you can identify the mountain in the background against the light sky, the large body of water, and the ragged shoreline in the foreground.

1 Here is another landscape collage from an advertisement in a magazine. What shapes can you identify?

landscape: *an arrangement of individual features or forms seen out-of-doors*

Cutting, Tearing, Folding, and Fastening Activities

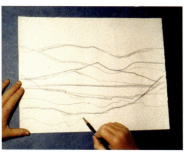

2 To begin your torn paper landscape, first make a rough sketch of a landscape. You can use pictures from magazines to help you.

6 Continue gluing down all of the shapes.

3 Using your sketch as reference, draw your landscape lightly on a piece of sturdy paper. Select colors of scrap paper suitable for your landscape, as the student has done in the upper left picture. Remember that lighter colors in the sky and background shapes will give the illusion of space. Then, begin carefully tearing shapes from the paper that match the shapes on your drawing. Rough, jagged edges on some of the shapes will make them more interesting.

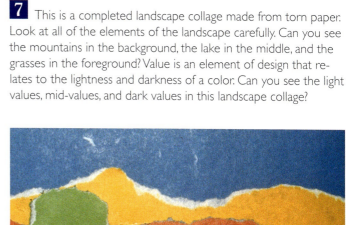

4 Arrange the shapes on the background paper. Start at the top and overlap the torn pieces of paper.

7 This is a completed landscape collage made from torn paper. Look at all of the elements of the landscape carefully. Can you see the mountains in the background, the lake in the middle, and the grasses in the foreground? Value is an element of design that relates to the lightness and darkness of a color. Can you see the light values, mid-values, and dark values in this landscape collage?

5 After you are pleased with your arrangement, glue down one piece at a time starting at the top.

8 Another collage uses some different landscape features. The tree shapes in the foreground are repeated in smaller sizes in the middle ground to give the illusion of depth. The road in the foreground leads your eye into the picture.

Art Activities with Paper, Clay, Fibers, and Printmaking: Using Masterworks as Inspiration

6 Shapes & Textures

Grade Level
5-6

Concept
Collage is an art technique in which materials such as paper, cloth, and/or found objects are fastened to a backing.

Skill
Organizing shapes of various textures into a composition.

Resource
Guitar, Georges Braque

Materials
Heavy paper or light cardboard; for backing: scissors, glue, staplers, and tape; cardboard templates of various sizes and shapes; (rectangles, triangles, circles, strips); many patterned and textured materials: papers of all kinds, fabrics, foil, leather scraps, shells, tiles, feathers, etc. (Wallpaper and drapery sample books are useful sources). "Treasured Trash" – beads, junk jewelry, buttons, etc.

Procedure
Prior to the art lesson, let students sort and classify the textured materials into groups—smooth, rough, bumpy, slippery, shiny, etc., to become familiar with the materials and their properties.

Study the resource collage to identify the materials that have been collaged as opposed to painted on. Notice that collages are organized into compositions. Clarify that "coller" (co-*lay*) is French for "to stick or glue" and mention that many 20th century artists made collages.

Students can draw rough compositions of different shapes to use as a guide when selecting materials. Demonstrate how to trace around a template laid on the reverse of a piece of material, cut out the shape, and place it with others on a background to create an interesting arrangement. Distribute everything but the glue, tape, and staplers and supervise students as they begin cutting, tearing, and arranging various textural materials. Encourage the use of occasional irregular shapes and small objects (shells, feathers) for variety.

When the compositions seem complete, have students fasten the pieces in place. A piece or two of carefully selected "Treasured Trash" may provide an accent to each collage composition.

Georges Braque, French, 1882-1963. *Guitar*, 1913. Cut-and-pasted printed and painted paper, charcoal, pencil, and gouache on gessoed canvas. 39¼ x 25⅝ inches (99.7 x 65.1 cm). Acquired through the Lillie P. Bliss Bequest. © 2011 Artists Rights Society (ARS), New York / ADAGP, Paris

This **collage** called *Guitar* was created by Georges Braque. Many artists have made collages with bits of natural and manufactured materials carefully arranged. Different kinds of papers have been fastened to a background in a composition. Both the background and the collage materials have been drawn on by the artist to furthur develop the image.

1 This collage was made by a young student. Shapes of various textures were organized into a composition. The shapes are all geometric – rectangular, square, triangular, and circular. Look at the textures. Do you think they are smooth, rough, bumpy, shiny, and slippery?

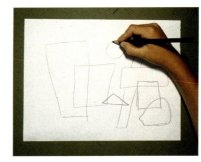

2 To begin this activity with collaging different shapes and textures, draw a rough composition of different shapes so that you will have a guide when selecting materials for your collage.

Cutting, Tearing, Folding, and Fastening Activities

collage: *art technique in which materials such as paper, cloth, or found objects are glued to a backing*

3 Select the textured materials you would like to use for your collage. Look at them and see the textures, then feel them. Do they feel the same way they appear? After your selection, begin cutting some of them in the shapes you have drawn on your background paper. The student in this picture has selected corrugated cardboard, a bumpy texture; leather, a smooth texture; fabric, a rough texture; and sandpaper, a scratchy texture.

4 Some of the textures can be torn into shapes. Here, sandpaper is being torn. Tearing creates a soft, ragged edge.

5 Begin arranging the textured materials on your drawn composition. Here, the bumpy corrugated cardboard is being placed on the drawing.

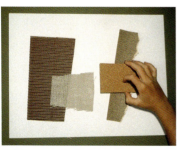

6 Overlap some of the shapes to create new shapes and color variation.

7 This student has cut a circle from a piece of shiny paper and arranged it in her composition.

8 When your composition of materials pleases you, you can glue the pieces in place.

9 Here is a completed collage. It is an abstract composition of shapes and textures. In this case, the work is abstract because it emphasizes the design of simple shapes. The variation of textures makes the design more interesting.

Art Activities with Paper, Clay, Fibers, and Printmaking: Using Masterworks as Inspiration

7 Texture Towers

Grade Level
5-8

Concept
1) Slotted cards may be fitted together to make a sculptural form; 2) Each card in the texture tower may represent a tactile quality and also, possibly, its visual counterpart.

Skill
Fastening without using glue or tape. Selecting a variation of textures.

Resource
House of Cards by Charles Eames

Materials
Sturdy cardboard; pencils or felt pens; scissors; paste, glue, staplers, tape, paper clips; many textural materials, e.g., carpet and drapery scraps, wallpaper samples, giftwrap, sandpaper, corrugated paper, foil, corkboard, foam rubber, styrofoam, patterned and textured fabrics; old magazines with examples of visual textures that match (an ad for bath towels and a piece of terry cloth).

Procedure
Before the lesson, prepare several cards for each student, as follows: Cut pieces of cardboard to a consistent size, approximately 6 x 9 inches. Cut out slits as indicated in the drawing, the thickness of the cardboard and about 1¼-inch long.

Look at *House of Cards*, noting the variety of patterns and how the pieces are interlocked.

Students will select a textured material and lay the cardboard as a pattern on the reverse side. They will trace around the card, indicate the location of the slits, and cut out the rectangular shape. They should check the length of the cardboard slits, then cut into the material to match. Next, they should choose the most effective fastening technique—glue, tape, staples, etc., and adhere the material to the card. (Part of the learning will be the experimentation at this step). If possible, search through old magazines and match the tactile texture with a picture of the same texture glued to the reverse of the card to show both tactile and visual surfaces.

As cards are completed, students will build a Texture Tower by interlocking the cards at the slits.

This cardboard sculpture is called *House of Cards* and was created by American designer Charles Eames (eems). Slotted cards were fitted together and interlocked to make the form. Notice that each card has a different visual **texture** and pattern. We will now explore creating a Texture Tower.

1 Your teacher will prepare several slotted cards for you like the blue one you see in this picture. Select different textures of materials to glue to the cards. Select many textures, scratchy, bumpy, rough — textures you can see as well as feel.

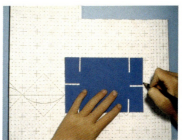

2 On the back of each material, draw around the slotted card, using it as a template, or drawing pattern.

texture: *the surface quality of materials, either tactile or visual*

Cutting, Tearing, Folding, and Fastening Activities

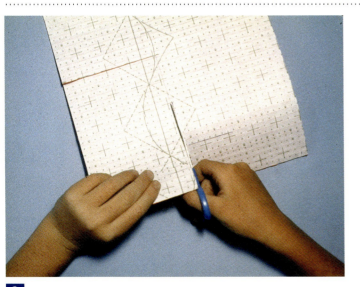

3 Cut out each textured or patterned material with scissors.

6 Begin assembling the tower by inserting the slots of one card into the slots of another card.

4 Then, glue the material to the slotted card to make it strong and sturdy enough to build a tower.

7 Alternate textures and patterns in the tower for visual and tactile interest. Tactile textures are textures you can feel.

5 Here are many textured cards students have made.

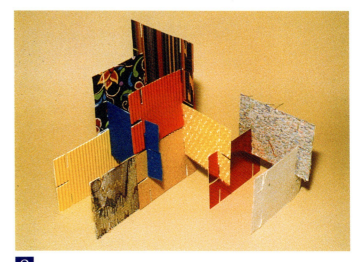

8 This is a completed Texture Tower. It is a sculptural form created by the unusual technique of fastening each card to another using slots. Can you describe the different textures?

Art Activities with Paper, Clay, Fibers, and Printmaking: Using Masterworks as Inspiration

8 Slot Sculpture

Grade Level
4-6

Concept
Flat shapes can be connected by notching.

Skill
Building forms from flat planes without glue.

Resource
Nessie by Rita Blitt

Materials
Thin cardboard or styrofoam; scissors; tempera paints and brushes; paper punch.

Procedure
Show the examples of Blitt's sculptures and explain that the large steel structure is called a stabile, in contrast to mobiles that are designed to move. The small paper maquette was cut from cardboard and slotted so it would stand freely.

Students draw, then cut cardboard in a variety of shapes and sizes, some with openings in them. Start the openings with a paper punch and enlarge with scissors. The shapes can be representational or nonobjective. They should paint the pieces on both sides with a limited array of colors, such as tints and shades of one color, contrasting, or analogous colors. Save some paint for touch-ups later. Cut one or more slots in each piece as it is combined with others in creating the sculpture. A stronger joining results if both pieces are slotted and interconnected. Occasionally transparent tape or a stapler may be needed. Evaluate finished sculptures in terms of originality and craftsmanship.

Note: Another resource might be Charles Eames's *House of Cards*, slotted rectangular cards that can be stacked. These have colorful surface patterns but only one shape and size.

Rita Blitt, American, born 1931. Nessie, 1890. Steel, 1978, 16 x 8 x 8 feet. Rockaway Town Square, Rockaway, New Jersey

This sculpture was created by contemporary American artist Rita Blitt and is called a **stabile**. Stabiles are stationary; they do not move as a mobile would. The sculpture is sixteen feet tall and was constructed of steel, then painted. The sculpture is called *Nessie* and it weighs 2,652 pounds.

1 This is a maquette that the artist made before creating the final sculpture. A maquette is a small scale model or rough draft of an architectural work or a sculpture.

stabile: *a freestanding abstract sculpture, typically of wire or sheet metal, in the style of a mobile but rigid and stationary*

Cutting, Tearing, Folding, and Fastening Activities

2 You can make a slot sculpture by first drawing two shapes on a piece of paper. One large shape will be the main part of the sculpture; the other will be a shape that will be inserted into the large shape to make it free-standing.

3 Cut out the shapes carefully.

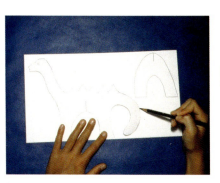

4 Place the cutout shapes on cardboard, and trace around them.

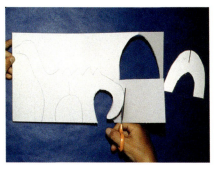

5 Cut out the shapes from the cardboard, making sure that you cut the slots in both.

6 Now, paint both pieces with bright colors.

7 After the shapes are dry, insert one slot into the other.

8 This is the completed "Slot Sculpture" standing freely. Use your imagination to create other stabiles. Draw a variety of shapes and sizes, and fit several more together.

21

Art Activities with Paper, Clay, Fibers, and Printmaking: Using Masterworks as Inspiration

9 Lines Create Shapes

Grade Level
4-6

Concept
A line is the edge of a shape.

Skill
Cutting and gluing complex shapes.

Resource
Red and Black by Henri Matisse, paper cutout. (Ahn-*ree* Mah-*teess*)

Materials
9 x 12-inch and 12 x 18-inch construction paper of contrasting colors; scissors; squeeze-bottles of glue.

Procedure
Look at Matisse's paper cutout and notice the organic shapes he has created with curving lines. Have the students draw a meandering line from one side of the paper to the other making sure the line doesn't cross itself. Then, they cut along the line and separate the shapes that result. Have them reassemble the pieces, each on one-half of the 12 x 18-inch paper, arranging them in a pleasing composition. The shapes can then be glued to the backing paper. Observe the nonobjective designs, comment on the positive and negative shapes, and display the colorful results.

Note: By using bright, complementary colors (red/green, yellow/violet, blue/orange), students can create optical effects similar to the work of painters of the Op Art period of the 1960s.

Henri Matisse, French, (1869-1954). *Composition, Black and Red*, 1947. Collage, 16 x 20¾ in. Davis Museum and Cultural Center, Wellesley College, Gift of Professor and Mrs. John McAndrew, 1958.11. © Scala/Art Resource, NY. © 2011 Succession H. Matisse / Artists Rights Society (ARS), New York

French artist Henri Matisse created many cutout collages in his later years. They were simple compositions made from pieces of brightly colored papers like the one you see here called *Composition, Black and Red*. Look at the left side. Can you see where one piece was cut out of another? The curving, organic shape relates to objects in nature. Look at the shape of the abstract figure on the right side. It too is an organic shape because it is made of irregular curving lines.

1 These images will help you recognize the difference between **organic shapes** and **geometric shapes**. On the left is a collage with organic shapes made with curving lines. On the right is a student work with geometric shapes made with straight lines and uniform shapes. It is helpful to remember that organic shapes are derived from nature, and geometric shapes are straight-edged with angles or circles and are usually derived from man-made objects.

geometric shapes: shapes with perfect, uniform measurements that don't often appear in nature

Cutting, Tearing, Folding, and Fastening Activities

2 The students here are drawing and cutting out organic shapes using a plant as a reference.

3 To discover how lines create shapes, draw a long, curving line from one corner of your paper to the opposite corner. Think about the plant leaf in the last picture. Make sure the line does not cross itself.

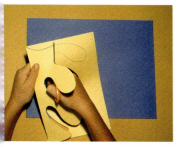

4 Now, cut your paper along the line you have drawn, then separate the two shapes.

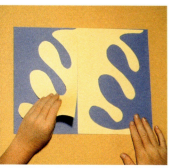

5 Arrange the two shapes on a larger piece of colored paper. Try them several ways. In this picture, the student has placed the shapes with their edges side by side. Can you see the positive and negative shapes that result? The yellow shape is the positive shape.

6 This is another way of arranging the shapes.

7 When you are satisfied with your composition, glue the shapes onto the background paper.

8 Here are four different compositions using exactly the same cutouts arranged in different ways. A composition is the way you arrange your subject matter.

9 Now try drawing other organic shapes by using curving lines. The seashells in this picture are organic because they were once alive and have a curving shape.

10 This student is arranging the positive and negative shapes she has drawn and cut out on a piece of background paper.

11 These are four examples of completed cutouts. They would all be considered abstract designs similar to the work of Matisse. Abstract art emphasizes design and simplifies or alters actual forms.

organic shapes: *shapes with a natural look and a flowing and curving appearance.*

Art Activities with Paper, Clay, Fibers, and Printmaking: Using Masterworks as Inspiration

10 Form: The Illusion of Volume

Grade Level
4-6

Concept
Shading produces the illusion of form, or volume.

Skill
Learning to shade cylinders and spheres and making a collage composition.

Resource
The Basket of Apples by Paul Cezanne (say-*zahn*)

Materials
12 x 18-inch gray or manila paper; scraps of colored construction paper; oil pastels; scissors; paste or glue.

Procedure
Look closely at the Cézanne still life. Analyze the colors and shapes and their placement in the painting. Determine how Cézanne shaded each object to make it appear solid. Note the use of highlights and the warm and cool colors. Warm hues seem to advance, cool ones to recede. Set up a still life of fruit or vegetables, pitcher, and drapery.

Have the students cut a circle from orange paper and compare it to one of Cézanne's fruits for the illusion of volume. Then, they should place a dot of white chalk for the highlight and use warm yellow and orange pastels to make a crescent around one edge and dark orange, blue, and violet around the opposite edge. From a distance, the paper circle should take on the illusion of a spherical fruit. Instruct students to cut the shapes of six fruits or vegetables, a pitcher or jug, and perhaps a plate from various colored scraps. They should compose an arrangement, overlapping the shapes on the larger paper and indicating the placement of the table and drapery. Then, piece by piece, using colors related to the cut shapes, they will shade each one and reassemble the composition.

The coloring of the table, cloth, and background will be added after the still life shapes have been touch-glued down. The rendering of cast shadows will complete the picture.

Paul Cézanne, French, 1839-1906. *The Basket of Apples*, c. 1893. Oil on canvas, 25 7/16 x 31 1/2 in. (65 x 80 cm). Helen Birch Bartlett Memorial Collection, 1926.252. The Art Institute of Chicago.

French artist Paul Cézanne was interested in painting objects to have an illusion of volume, or solid **form**. The painting here is called *The Basket of Apples*. Notice how the shading and highlights on the fruit make it appear solid. These elements create an illusion of volume in the painting as well as his use of warm and cool colors. Do you remember that warm hues seem to advance and cool ones seem to recede?

1 To explore creating volume in your artwork, begin by studying a still life arrangement set up in your classroom. Study the forms of the fruit, vegetables, pitcher, and plate. You can see the highlights and shadows which create the illusion of volume.

form: describes objects that are three-dimensional, having length, width, and height

Cutting, Tearing, Folding, and Fastening Activities

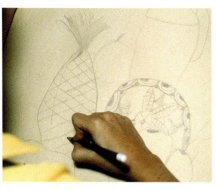

2 Draw some of the objects in the still life. Observe their texture as well as their form.

3 After you have practiced drawing some of the objects and have their shape and size in mind, begin cutting their shapes out of different colored papers.

4 Use oil pastels to create shadows and highlights. A spot of white on an orange creates a highlight. Yellow and orange at one edge and dark orange, blue, and violet on the opposite edge make it look three-dimensional.

5 Remember to color in the lines or texture on the objects.

6 Notice the shading and highlights on the lemons and oranges. Finishing details are being applied to the pineapple.

7 Arrange the shapes on a background paper. Be sure to overlap some of the shapes. This creates not only a better design but an illusion of depth. When you are pleased with the arrangement, glue the shapes in place.

8 The coloring of the table and background can be added after the glue has dried. Draw in some cast shadows to complete the illusion of volume.

9 Here are four other examples of finished work. Look carefully at all the elements in each picture which make the objects appear to have form.

25

Art Activities with Paper, Clay, Fibers, and Printmaking: Using Masterworks as Inspiration

11 A Haiku Book

Grade Level
5-6

Concept
Art can be functional.

Skill
Measuring, folding, cutting, gluing.

Resource
Japanese Haiku books

Materials
Dip-dyed rice paper, grasscloth wallpaper, wrapping paper, or plain paper for stamping, 2 pieces 6 x 6 inches; potatoes for stamps; table knife; tempera paint; two pieces of cardboard, 5 x 5 inches; one strip of shelf paper 4½ x 36 inches; glue or paste; two pieces of ¼-inch ribbon 12 inches long.

Procedure
The photograph shows a display of Japanese Haiku books. "Haiku" means a short Japanese poem, and they are traditionally written in books such as these. The books are decorated with prints, paintings, or drawings.

If the students are to decorate the papers, have them cut potato stamps and print book covers with tempera paint. Then, they should place a square of cardboard in the center of the wrong side of one of the 6 x 6-inch printed, patterned, or dip-dyed papers. A dot of glue should be placed on each corner of the cardboard and the paper folded over to make a neat, equilateral triangle. A fine line of glue is trailed along next to each edge of the paper which is then folded carefully over the cardboard. The diagonals should meet to form mitered corners. The long paper is then folded in half, fourths, and eighths, creasing accurately. It is then opened and refolded like an accordian (fan-fold). If desired, one end of a ribbon could be glued to each cardboard with 8 inches extending over the edge, left or right. The students should then trail glue or paste about ½ inch from every edge of the 4½-inch square on the end of the strip and place it in the center of the cardboard so that the ribbon extends from the side, not the top, as the pages fold and open. Repeat with the other end of the strip, matching the ribbons, making sure that both covers are aligned and the folded pages are accurately enclosed. Place under a weight until the glue is dry.

Japanese Haiku Books

This picture shows a display of Japanese Haiku books. "Haiku" means a short Japanese poem, and they are traditionally written in books such as these. The books are decorated with prints, paintings, or drawings.

1 These are the materials needed to make a Haiku book — printed covers, cardboard, end papers, and a long strip of paper to be folded to fit the inside of the book. Here, a stamp has been made to print the covers of the book.

2 A student cuts a potato into the shape he desires to make a stamp to print the cover papers. He stamps the potato into red ink and presses it on the paper, creating an allover **pattern**.

Cutting, Tearing, Folding, and Fastening Activities

6 Then, glue the other end to the end paper of the other cover.

3 Other shapes and colors can be used to print the covers.

7 You can see how the folded paper fits inside the book. Place the book under a weight until the glue is dry.

8 When the glue is dry, the ribbons can be tied together to make the completed book.

4 Apply glue to a piece of cardboard and place the cardboard over the reverse side of the printed paper so that the borders are even. Put a dot of glue on each corner of the cardboard, and fold the paper over to make a triangle. Apply glue along each edge and fold the paper carefully over the cardboard.

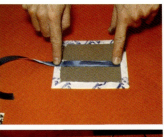

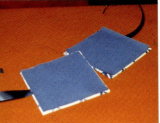

9 Here are examples of Haiku books that students made. Your book can be used for writing poems or painting small pictures.

5 To complete your cover, place a line of glue across the center of the cardboard and put a piece of ribbon on it. Glue a piece of colored paper over the cardboard and the ribbon. Do the same for the other cover. Now, accordion fold a piece of long, narrow paper. Place a line of glue around the edge of one end.

pattern: **elements repeated over and over, arranged in a predetermined sequence**

Art Activities with Paper, Clay, Fibers, and Printmaking: Using Masterworks as Inspiration

12 Scribbles and Nibbles: Tear into Action

Grade Level
6-8

Concept
The human figure in action is a subject of artists.

Skill
Gesture drawing; tearing and fastening.

Resource
Snap the Whip by Winslow Homer

Materials
Colored paper 9 x 12 inches and 12 x 18 inches; crayons or felt pens; glue or paste.

Procedure
Look at Homer's painting and call attention to the many diagonals and resulting triangles. Notice the position of the heads in relation to the torsos of the figures in action. Encourage some students to assume these poses and the poses of other sports and games while others analyze the action lines.

With crayons or marking pens, students will make a rapid gesture, or "scribble", drawing of a posed figure, or one from a painting. When five or six gesture drawings of different poses have been made, each will be torn from the papers with tiny, controlled nibbling tears, not rips. Turned over to hide the scribbles, the figures are arranged on a larger sheet of paper of contrasting color and fastened down with a minimal amount of glue applied to the scribbled side. Details can then be added to show the environment, if desired.

Note: Another day, have the students tear the figures directly from the classified ad section of the newspaper without drawing first. Have them also use plain white paper. Then, they can arrange two or more figures overlapping on a black background. Silhouette the posed students against a bright window to make the contour outline easier to see.

Winslow Homer, American, 1836-1910. *Snap the Whip (Snapping the Whip)*, 1872. Oil on canvas, 22 x 36 inches (55.88 x 91.44 cm). Butler Institute of American Art, Youngstown, OH

American artist Winslow Homer created this painting called *Snap the Whip*. It depicts children in the act of playing a game. Notice the position of the heads in relation to the bodies. Can you see the diagonals and the resulting triangles? In this experience, you will learn how to show figures in action.

1 Some students in your class can pose for your drawing. Here, girls pose with a soccer ball. Dancing, running, jumping, kicking a football could be other poses.

2 With rapid gesture, or "scribble" drawing, make several drawings of different poses. You can see how **gesture drawing** is done in this picture. Use different colors of paper, and be sure to draw different action poses.

Cutting, Tearing, Folding, and Fastening Activities

gesture drawing: *fluid, loose line drawings made quickly to show a subject in motion*

3 Can you see the movement in these gesture drawings? Be sure and study your posed models to see where the arms come out of the body and the relation and proportion of each part of the body to the other.

4 Each drawing can now be torn from the papers with tiny, controlled "nibbling" tears, not rips.

5 Small tears, or nibbles, will enable you to remove even the smallest part of the figure from the paper.

7 Remember too that warm colors in the foreground and cool colors in the background create an illusion of depth. The student here has placed a soccer ball near the foot of one of his figures to further emphasize the action.

8 When you're satisfied with the composition, glue the figures to the colored background paper.

6 Turn the figures over to hide the scribbles, and arrange them on a piece of colored paper. Overlap the figures so they look like they are actually playing a game.

9 Here is a student's completed picture. The figures appear to be very active. Can you see the diagonal shapes which show movement?

Art Activities with Paper, Clay, Fibers, and Printmaking: Using Masterworks as Inspiration

13 Wycinanki

Grade Level
6-8

Concept
People of many cultures create folk art with cut paper designs.

Skill
Precise folding, cutting, and fastening of symmetrical shapes.

Resource
Wycinanki (paper cutout) by Czeslawa Konopka. (vee-chee-*non*-key)

Materials
Bright-colored lightweight paper; sharp scissors; black, white, or contrasting colors of construction paper or matboard for mounting; white glue; scratch paper for planning designs.

Procedure
Analyze the example noting the symmetrical design and precise cutting.

Have the students plan a symmetrical design of natural elements, flowers, trees, roosters or other birds, farm animals, or people, and make a drawing. Then, they fold the colored paper in half and draw one-half of their design with the center on the fold, using the full height and width of the paper. Have them make certain the design will be one connected piece when opened. They should plan for some interior cuts where the double thickness must be pierced and cut away to make solid areas more open and also look at the edges and determine which can be enhanced later with zigzag or scalloped cuts. They could shade with pencil all areas that are to be cut away to avoid any mistaken cuts, and make a final check to see that all of the parts are connected to the central spine. Then, they can cut out the baseline and the general outline first, decorate the edges and cut away interior parts by punching a hole, inserting scissor tips, and clipping to the interior outline. Large leaf or flower shapes could be folded at this point and further decorative edges or interior cuts can be made.

Open the wycinanki and use glue sparingly to mount it onto a rectangle of white, black, or colored paper. Mount this paper on a still larger one of the same color as the wycinanki.

Czeslawa Konopka, Polish, *Wycinanka*

People of many cultures create folk art with cut-paper designs. The Polish version of this tradition is called **wycinanki**. It is the result of precise folding and cutting of symmetrical shapes and is a Polish tradition. Each year, Polish families make these forms, mount them, and hang them in their homes for decoration.

1 To begin your wycinanki activity, plan, then sketch symmetrical designs of natural elements: flowers, trees, animals, and people.

wycinanki: the art of Polish papercutting

Cutting, Tearing, Folding, and Fastening Activities

2 Fold a piece of colored paper in half, and draw one-half of your design with the center on the fold. Use the full height and width of your paper. Be sure the design will be a single, connected piece when opened. Plan some interior cuts, where the paper must be pierced and cut away, to make solid areas more open.

3 Now, carefully cut your design out of the folded paper. Cut the large shapes first.

4 After the design is cut out, additional decoration can be added. Keep the paper folded and snip out small designs.

5 Now, open your design and arrange it on another piece of colored paper of the same size from which your design was cut. Lift sections of the design and glue them to secure it to the paper.

6 Notice how symmetrical, or evenly balanced, this wycinanki design is because it was cut from the folded paper.

7 Here are two other examples of wycinanki to give you inspiration for your own designs.

31

Art Activities with Paper, Clay, Fibers, and Printmaking: Using Masterworks as Inspiration

14 Cardboard Weaving

Grade Level
4-6

Concept
A woven fabric consists of warp and weft threads.

Skill
Learning basic tabby (over-under) weaving.

Resource
Landscape by Carolyn Hedstrom

Materials
Cardboard, 12 x 12 inches; scissors; colored string or carpet warp; many colored and textured yarns, 1-inch wide strips of fabric, ribbon, pipe cleaner chenille, raffia, natural materials, cut to 12-inch lengths; masking tape.

Procedure
Look at the weaving example and explain that it is a fabric woven with yarn by hand on a loom.

Students prepare looms with the 12-inch squares of cardboard by cutting into two opposite edges a series of 1/4-inch slashes about 1/2 inch apart. The children warp each loom with string. 26 foot balls of string could be rolled for each child.

To warp the loom: Fasten one end of the string on the back of the cardboard with tape and bring it to the front through the cut nearest the corner. Catch it through the comparable cut across the loom, then bring it forward again through the next notch and back to the first edge. Continue "crossing and catching," not wrapping around the loom, until it is covered with parallel lines of warp. Fasten the string on back with tape. The string should lie flat without buckling the loom.

If students have no previous weaving experience, stand six or eight students in a row, arm's length apart, to represent the warp strings. A weaver (the weft yarn) moves in and out from one end to the other, to demonstrate the over-under, basic "tabby" weave technique. Another weft weaver should move across, out and in, representing the alternate row of weaving.

Then, children select a variety of colored and textured weft materials and begin weaving. Pattern may be emphasized, e.g., ABCCBA, or free exploration of textures and colors. Each weft should be pushed up close to the preceding one.

Carolyn Hedstrom, American, 1853–1890. *Landscape.* Weaving.

This is a weaving by American artist Carolyn Hedstrom. She weaves different colors and textures of fibers, interlacing them on a loom, and the result is a woven fabric. In this activity, you will learn basic over-under weaving, called "tabby" weaving.

1 To make your loom, a frame for interlacing fibers, begin by making 1/2-inch marks across the top and bottom of a piece of cardboard using a ruler. Then cut quarter-inch slashes at each of the marks you have made.

2 Using string, begin to warp your loom. The warp is the string through which you weave your yarn. Tape the end of the string to the back of the cardboard and run it through the first slash. Bring it down to the bottom and back up again, all across the cardboard. The string should lie flat and snug without buckling the cardboard.

warp: the set of lengthwise yarns through which the weft is woven

Fibers and Designing Activities

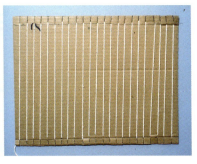

3 This is the warped loom. Secure the string on the back of the cardboard with tape.

weft: *the horizontal threads that are interlaced through the warp in a woven fabric*

4 Now, you will begin to weave the weft materials, pieces of colored and textured yarn. With the end of the yarn, weave under the first warp string, then over the second, under the third, and so forth across the loom. Then another row of either the same or different weft yarn is woven through the warp. Each weft should be pushed up close to the one before it, and you can use a wide-toothed comb to help you.

8 Now that you understand the process, you can experiment with different textures such as ribbons, yarns, raffia, or natural materials, as the student is doing here.

5 You may change colors of yarn throughout your weaving in a free exploration of a design. This variation would add interest.

9 You can see the interesting design being woven here.

6 Be sure to cut the ends of the yarn evenly. The ends can be left to hang freely from your weaving or be brought to the back and taped.

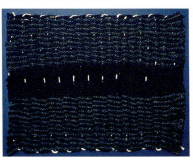

7 This is a completed weaving. Notice that this student has used variation in his choice of colors. Also, he has made a more interesting design by allowing the warp to show through in a band across the center.

10 This is the completed weaving. Because color and texture are elements of design, this student has created an attractive work of art which is mounted on a mat for display.

15 Yarn Paintings

Grade Level
4-6

Concept
Colored fibers can make unusual "paintings."

Skill
Making a yarn painting simulating a Huichol technique.

Resource
Huichol (*wee*-chole) yarn painting

Materials
Stiff cardboard 9 x 12 inches; medium-weight yarns of many colors; scissors; toothpicks; glue in small applicator bottles.

Procedure
Explain that the Huichol people of Northern Mexico, descendants of the Aztecs, press yarns closely together into sunwarmed beeswax to make decorative plaques. They used symbols from religion and myths to create this unique art form. Look at the example and notice the simplified, abstract shapes.

Have the students make a sketch of a simple shape, animal, bird, fish, flower, butterfly, etc., and transfer it to the cardboard. Then the outline is traced with glue from an applicator tip and yarn pressed on top of it. Use a small ball of yarn so as not to run short, then clip off the extra yarn. Repeat for the rest of the drawn lines. Each shape is filled in, one at a time, starting with a line of glue next to the outline and working toward the center. Choose bright, contrasting colors. When the shapes are complete, the background is filled in with a different color. All of the cardboard should be covered.

Around the very edge of the rectangle, a frame is made with different colors of yarn, nudging each color up to the next with a toothpick. Mount the finished yarn painting on colored construction paper or cardboard.

Huichol yarn painting

This is an example of a Huichol yarn painting. The Huichol people of Mexico press yarn into sun-warmed beeswax to make religious offerings to local gods as well as decorative artwork to sell. Notice the simplified, abstract shapes of natural subjects which are unrealistic in color.

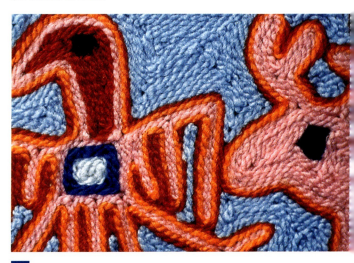

1 In this detail, you can see how the yarn is pressed very closely together into the waxed surface. Notice also how they outlined their figures with several colors of yarn for more emphasis.

Huichol: indigenous people of west central Mexico, living in the Sierra Madre Occidental range in the Mexican states of Nayarit, Jalisco, Zacatecas, and Durango.

Fibers and Designing Activities

2 Let's now explore a more simplified way of creating a yarn painting similar to the Huichol people. First, look at pictures from magazines and books to get some ideas for the subject of your yarn painting.

3 Then, make a sketch of the subject you have selected on drawing paper.

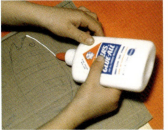 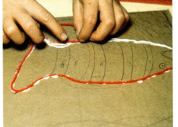

4 Transfer the drawing to a piece of cardboard, and trace the outline of your subject with a line of glue. Press a piece of yarn on top of the glue line.

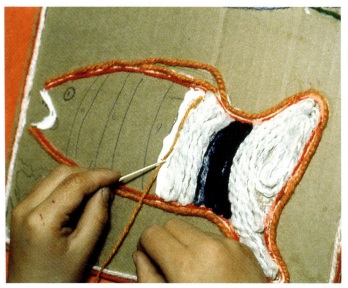

5 Fill in each shape, starting with a line of glue next to the outline and pressing in one row of yarn at a time. Use a toothpick to help push each row of yarn close to another. Try not to get glue on the upper surface of the yarn. Use bright, contrasting colors.

6 When the main shape is complete, fill in the background. Here, blue and green yarn have been alternated in a wavy fashion to simulate water. Around the edge of the cardboard, make a neat "frame" with several colors of yarn.

7 Here is the completed yarn painting. It looks very much like the Huichol yarn paintings made with yarn pressed into beeswax. Also, the shape is simple with bright colors, and the texture of the yarn makes it an interesting painting.

Art Activities with Paper, Clay, Fibers, and Printmaking: Using Masterworks as Inspiration

16 Paper Mask

Grade Level
5-6

Concept
Masks are symmetrical designs derived from facial features.

Skill
Designing a three-dimensional mask of paper.

Resource
African Mask

Materials
Black construction paper 12 x 18 inches; white chalk; oil pastels (or art chalk and fixative); scissors; stapler or glue; yarn.

Procedure
Look at the masks and notice the distortions and exaggerations of the basic features.

Placing the paper vertically, have the children sketch three large, geometric shapes in any order, overlapping a circle, a rectangle, a triangle. At least one should fill the entire width of the paper. Then, the shapes are redrawn lightly with white chalk on the black paper. Next, the outside of the shapes is outlined to establish the overall shape of the mask. The two sides should be lightly folded together to find the midline and an elongated geometric shape for a nose is drawn. Exaggerated eyes, not necessarily to see through, and a mouth with expression, a scowl, snarl, smirk, sneer, or snicker should be drawn. Scars, wrinkles, or magic symbols are added. Oil pastels or art chalk are used for bright color. Art chalk must be sprayed with fixative outdoors by the teacher.

The mask is cut around the outside. Two one-inch slashes can be made at the top and the bottom corners overlapping the edges to make the mask three-dimensional, and staple or glue. Add feathers, raffia, or yarn, as desired.

Extension: If the mask is to be worn, make holes where eyes can see through, reinforce the sides with masking tape on the back, paper-punch holes, and tie with thick, colorful yarn or raffia.

Transformation mask. Cedar wood. Shown in open position. Kwakiutl. © The Field Museum, # A108352c

Masks conceal or disguise a face. This mask is a North American Native American mask. The mask was designed with abstract and geometric shapes which distort human features. Masks are used in traditional dances, religious ceremonies, and many years ago, were worn by warriors to disguise the tribe from which they came. Notice that the design on the mask is symmetrical; both sides of the mask are the same.

mask: *a covering for all or part of the face, used for protection or decoration*

1 To design a mask, first make a drawing of three large, geometric shapes overlapping each other on a piece of paper. Geometric shapes are circles, triangles, rectangles, or squares. At least one shape should fill the entire width of the paper. Sketch in lightly some exaggerated facial features.

Fibers and Designing Activities

2 On black construction paper, redraw the shapes with white chalk. Can you identify the three geometric shapes drawn here?

5 Now, cut the mask out of the paper.

3 Draw exaggerated eyes and a nose. Make a mouth that shows expression. Add magic symbols or scars.

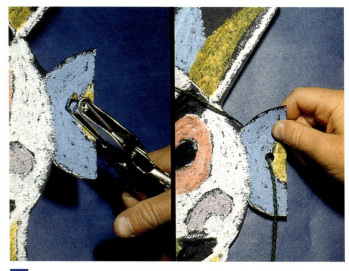

6 To wear the mask, punch one hole in each ear and insert a length of string for tying together around the head.

4 Color the shapes with bright oil pastels or chalk. Because your design is symmetrical, the colors on one side of the mask should be the same as those on the other.

7 A student is wearing her finished mask. Compare her mask with the Native American mask on the right.

Transformation mask. Cedar wood. Shown in open position. Kwakiutl. © The Field Museum, # A108351c

Art Activities with Paper, Clay, Fibers, and Printmaking: Using Masterworks as Inspiration

17 Banners

Grade Level
5-8

Concept
Banners incorporate symbols, borders, and letters to give a message.

Skill
Designing a personal banner with cut paper.

Resource
Banners at Art Museum.

Materials
12 x 18-inch colored construction or Fadeless paper; felt pens; scissors; glue; dowels; yarn.

Procedure
Look at the example and talk about the purposes of banners and their use of symbols and decorative borders.

Have the children choose three colors of paper, a main color for the banner and different colors for the letters and symbols. They draw the letters of one word or a short phrase large and widely spaced with a felt pen. The letters are cut out, arranged, and glued on the banner.

Borders are made by doubling a piece of paper the width of the banner. Scoops or notches are cut along the edge. The border is glued to the banner, front and back, allowing room to insert a dowel for hanging. Add another border with slashes cut for fringe to the bottom. Trimmings of paper, foil, or yarn can be added to enhance the banner.

Symbols can be cut, arranged, and glued to the banner. Insert dowel rod and hang the banner with yarn or cord.

Banners use symbols, borders, and letters to give a message. The banners seen here hang in front of an Art Museum and have artistic images and shapes on them. Many times, banners are used to announce the opening of an art show, a circus, or a rodeo.

1 Let's explore making a paper banner similar to the ones you just saw. Choose three colors of paper. In the picture you see here, red will be the background color of the banner. Do you remember that red is a ***primary color***?

2 Draw large letters spelling your message on another color. In this case, it is yellow, another primary color.

Fibers and Designing Activities

3 Cut out each letter carefully.

4 Arrange the letters in a good design that can be easily read. Next, lift each letter, apply glue, and replace it on the banner.

5 To make a decorative border, fold a piece of paper in half. Cut scoops or notches on the edge. Open the border and glue it to the front and back of the banner leaving a space under the fold to insert a dowel rod for hanging.

6 On another piece of paper, cut slashes on one side, and glue it to the bottom of the banner. This will create a fringe.

primary colors: *three main colors (red, yellow, and blue) that can be combined to make all other colors*

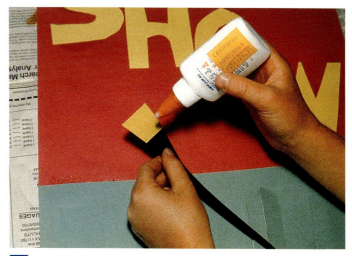

7 For further decoration, this student cut out shapes of paint brushes and glued them on the banner.

8 Here is the completed banner announcing an art show. Could you design a banner for an event at your school?

Art Activities with Paper, Clay, Fibers, and Printmaking: Using Masterworks as Inspiration

18 Adinkra Prints

Grade Level
6-8

Concept
Block printing can be used to decorate textiles.

Skill
Relief printing on fabric.

Resource
Adinkra cloth from Ghana (ah-*dink*-rah)

Materials
One-inch slices of potato; table knives; styrofoam meat trays; scissors; pencils; small blocks of wood; glue; black tempera paint; ½-inch stiff bristle brushes; strips of cardboard; newspapers; 12-inch squares of bright-colored cloth or a large piece of cloth.

Procedure
Look at example and explain that adkinkra cloth is printed with designs having symbolic meaning to the people of Ghana, Africa, and it is made into clothing that is traditionally worn for special occasions. Their stamps are carved from calabashes and dipped into a dye made from tree bark. The cloth is divided into squares by a comb dipped into the dye, and a different symbol is stamped in each square. Sometimes, long strips of cloth are printed and stitched together with bright, contrasting thread.

Children will cut a symbol from a piece of styrofoam, or a potato may be used, adding details by pressing firmly with a pencil, and gluing the styrofoam to a small block of wood or empty thread spool. Practice printing a design on newspaper before attempting it on the cloth.

Divide the cloth into segments with an inked comb. Brush the paint onto the styrofoam or potato with a flat brush held at a low angle to keep the paint out of the grooves. Stamp on the cloth over a thick pad of newspapers. If cloth is to be washed, use acrylic paint.

Wash brushes well immediately after using them with acrylic paint. Oil-based printing ink and a brayer can be substituted, but cleanup will require turpentine or mineral spirits.

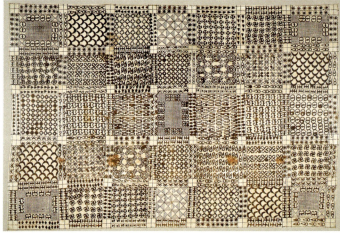

Wrapper, Asante peoples, Ghana, Mid-late 19th century. Imported cotton cloth, black pigment, 76⁹⁄₁₆ × 112⁷⁄₁₆ inches (194.5 × 285.6 cm). Museum purchase, 83-3-8. Photograph by Franko Khoury. National Museum of African Art, Smithsonian Institution

This is an **Adinkra** cloth which was made in Ghana, West Africa. "Adinkra" is the name of the black dye made from the bark of a tree. It is pressed onto cloth with a stamp. Notice how the cloth is divided into squares, each printed with a single symbol.

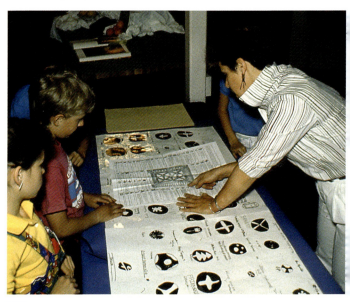

1 In this picture, a teacher is pointing out Adinkra symbols to students. Each symbol has a different meaning, such as Wisdom, Defender of the King, and many, many others.

Adinkra: symbols, originally created in West Africa, that represent concepts or motifs. Used on fabric, pottery, woodcarvings, and logos.

Fibers and Designing Activities

2 To begin this activity, divide a large cloth into squares by pulling an inked cardboard comb horizontally and vertically across the cloth. Or, a felt pen and yardstick can also be used.

5 Then, each student will stamp his symbol in rows on a square.

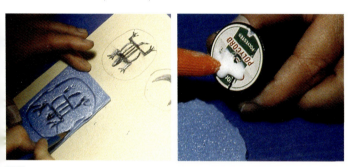

3 Practice drawing symbols on a piece of paper. Select a symbol and draw it on a small piece of styrofoam, pressing firmly with a pencil. Cut out and glue the stamp to an empty thread spool.

6 Students should re-ink their stamp as often as necessary to make sure their prints are clear. These students are completing their Adinkra cloth.

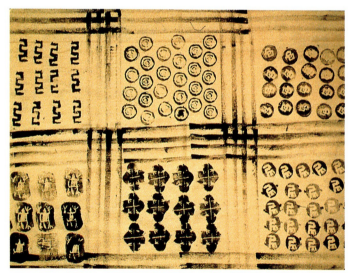

4 The stamps are then brushed with black acrylic paint.

7 This is a detail from the larger cloth. Each square has a different symbol printed on it, and the children have made up a meaning for each one based on their study of Adinkra symbolism.

Art Activities with Paper, Clay, Fibers, and Printmaking: Using Masterworks as Inspiration

19 Paper Molas

Grade Level
6–8

Concept
People use design motifs to decorate clothing.

Skill
Simulating a Panamanian craft with paper.

Resource
Kuna (Panama) mola panel

Materials
Assorted colors 9 x 12-inch construction paper or felt; pencils; scissors; glue; newspapers.

Procedure
Look at the example and explain that molas have traditionally been made by the Kuna people living on an island off the coast of Panama. With the technique of reverse-applique, fabric of cutout openings placed over a contrasting background to expose the second color, they made designs to decorate their clothing. By using multiple layers, each cutout exposing more layers beneath, intricate designs were made. Older students can simulate this technique with paper or felt. Younger ones can create similar designs with the usual add-on applique method rather than the more difficult cutting away.

Younger students: Draw the shape of an animal, bird, or butterfly on colored paper. Cut it out and place it on another colored paper. Draw around the shape leaving about a 1/4-inch border. Cut out the second shape and glue the two together. Do the same on a third colored paper, cut, and glue. Then, the shapes are glued to the center of a larger piece of colored paper, and small decorative strips added.

Older students: Draw the outline of a single animal, bird, or butterfly in the center of colored paper. Draw rows of long, narrow ovals to fill the background space. Cut out each shape carefully with a knife or scissors. Lay this sheet on top of the second color and draw a slightly smaller version inside it. Cut out this shape and lay it on a third color and repeat the process. Stack all three cutouts on uncut colored paper. By cutting out corner sections of the middle sheets, the colors of the background pattern are changed, or use small scraps of color to slip beneath some of the ovals. Glue the sheets together.

Mola, Cuna Indians, Panama

Molas were originally made by the Kuna people living on an island off the coast of Panama. Several layers of different colored fabric with cutout shapes are placed over a background color. Molas traditionally decorate clothing.

1 We will demonstrate how you can make molas on paper. First, practice drawing an animal, bird, or butterfly shape.

2 Choose one of the shapes and redraw it on colored paper. Then, cut out the shape. Place it on another piece of paper of a different color. Draw around the shape leaving about a quarter-inch border.

Fibers and Designing Activities

3 Cut out the second shape, then glue the two together.

4 On a third piece of colored paper, draw around the two glued shapes, again leaving a border, and cut out the shape. Glue this shape to the bottom of the first two.

6 An older child is starting to make a paper mola a different way. After the shape is drawn, she cuts it out. Rows of long, narrow ovals are also cut out in the background space.

7 The cutout sheet is placed on top of a second color and a smaller version of the shape is drawn about a quarter inch inside the first shape. Then, the second shape is cut out. A third color is placed underneath the first two cutout sheets.

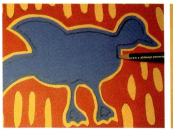

8 Again, a smaller version of the shape is drawn and cut out. Now, all the sheets are placed on another color. You can see the pink paper beneath the cutout sheets here.

5 The shapes are then glued to a large piece of paper of a different color, and small strips of color are added for decoration.

mola: *a textile made by sewing layers of colored cloth together to form patterns*

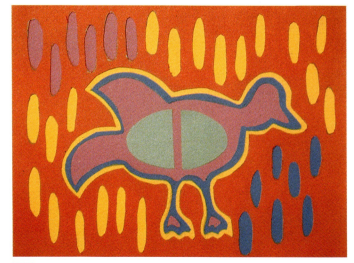

9 Notice the different colors behind the background ovals because parts of the background sheets were cut away. This paper mola has an intricate design very similar to a Kuna mola.

43

Art Activities with Paper, Clay, Fibers, and Printmaking: Using Masterworks as Inspiration

20 Name Patterns

Grade Level
4-6

Concept
Letter shapes can be used as design elements.

Skill
Creating a pattern by using letter shapes.

Resource
Once Emerged from the Gray of Night by Paul Klee (clay)

Materials
One-inch graph paper, 9 x 12 inches; pencils; crayons; watercolor paints and brushes; water containers; paint rags; newspapers

Procedure
Show the example and tell the students that the Swiss artist Paul Klee is credited with originating this graphic design technique. On a small sheet of paper, he drew a grid and then printed a poem, one letter to a space, covering the area completely. He finished the design by adding watercolors to the shapes that resulted between the letters. This lesson modifies the idea for children.

Less mature students can achieve good results by printing their names in all capital letters, each letter filling one square, and stacking row on row to make a vertical pattern. A more sophisticated design will result from a stair-stepped beginning, moving the first letter over one square in each subsequent row. A little study will reveal how to fill in the empty blocks to the left. All the letters should be capitals, upper case, and should "bump the sides" of the squares, except "I." When the design is complete, the students use watercolors. Younger children paint a simple watercolor wash with a contrasting color. Older students find areas to paint bounded by pencil lines, and use several colors, repeating the patterns down the page.

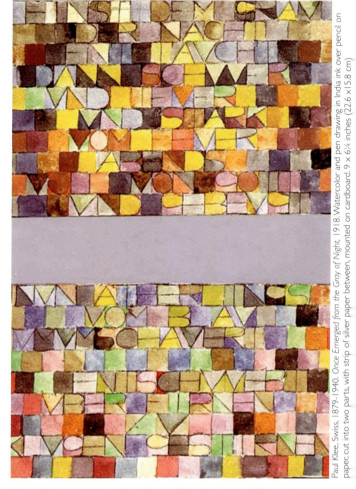

Paul Klee, Swiss, 1879-1940. *Once Emerged from the Gray of Night*, 1918. Watercolor and pen drawing in India ink over pencil on paper, cut into two parts, with strip of silver paper between, mounted on cardboard. 9 x 6¼ inches (22.6 x 15.8 cm)

Once Emerged from the Gray of Night by Paul Klee shows how he used a **graphic design** technique to create a painting. On a sheet of paper, he drew a grid and then printed a poem, one letter to a square. He finished the design by adding watercolors to the shapes created by the letters.

1 Let's explore using letter shapes as design elements. First, draw a grid using a ruler to make one-inch squares.

Fibers and Designing Activities

graphic design: *a creative process which combines words, symbols, and images to create a visual representation of ideas and messages*

2 Print each letter of your name in capital letters in the squares with a crayon or pencil. Print your name over and over again until the letters fill the entire grid. Make sure the letters touch the tops and sides of the squares, except for the letter "I" which should be placed in the center of the square. Use only capital letters.

3 After you've completed the grid, drop water in all the colors of your watercolor palette.

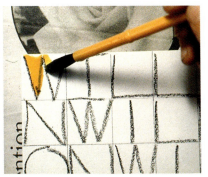

4 The spaces created around the letters are negative spaces. Paint all of these shapes.

5 Vary the colors. Use contrasting colors next to each other.

6 Try painting warm and cool colors next to each other, too. Warm colors are in the families of yellows, reds, and oranges, and cool colors are in the families of blues, greens, and purples.

7 Notice the design that is being created here by using the same colors in the negative spaces of the letters.

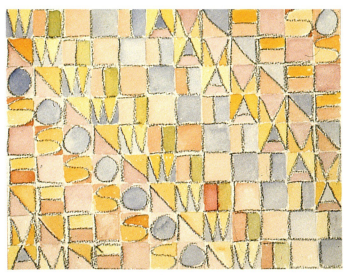

8 Can you find the design made by the colors in the completed painting here? The shapes and lines have also made a design. Color, shape, and line are elements of design.

21 Quilt Blocks

Grade Level
4-6

Concept
Geometric shapes repeated to form patterns have been used to enhance functional objects.

Skill
Designing quilt blocks based on geometric shapes and simple grids.

Resource
Fanfare by Molly Upton

Materials
Six-inch squares of white paper; two-inch squares of colored paper; rulers; scissors; pencils; glue.

Procedure
Show Upton's quilt and the student example. Comment that quilts were made by Colonial Americans from scraps left over from homespun and woven cloth used for clothing. It was a social activity, too, to piece and quilt bedcoverings. Archaeologists have discovered ancient quilting, including a jacket worn by an Egyptian pharoah around 3400 BC. Marco Polo introduced quilts to Europe about 1200 AD, and the Crusaders found quilting in the Middle East about the same time and discovered that it made good armor.

Students will design nine-patch blocks using paper; however, any number can be made. Distribute 6-inch squares of white paper and two colors of the 2-inch squares. Students will measure and mark the white squares into nine 2-inch squares. The colored squares are to be divided into triangles by cutting each diagonally once or twice, or 1-inch squares, or 1 x 2-inch rectangles. When sufficient numbers of pieces have been cut, students should explore a variety of arrangements, trying for an original, unique design. They may wish to give their patterns names, as Colonial quilters did. Carefully glue each pattern to the white background.

All of the blocks may be taped together on the back and displayed as a paper quilt, similar to the "sampler" quilts often made by young people in Colonial times.

Molly Upton, American, 1953-1976. *Fanfare*, 1975. Quilt, 118½ x 80½ inches. American Craft Council, Minneapolis, MN

This is a quilt called *Fanfare* made by American artist Molly Upton. Sewing together triangles of cloth of the same size, she created a surface of many colors with a glowing center of interest. Quilted materials have been made by people for thousands of years to be used for clothing and bed coverings. It is still a social activity where several people each make patterned squares, then join them together to make a large quilt.

1 This is a paper quilt design several students made. Each student designed several squares with **geometric shapes** that were than assembled and fastened into one large composition. Let's learn how this was done.

geometric shapes: shapes that are precise and regular, i.e. squares, circles, triangles, rectangles, etc.

Fibers and Designing Activities

2 Make two-inch marks all around a six-inch square of paper using a ruler.

3 Draw lines between the marks to make nine squares on the paper.

4 Now, cut two-inch squares of paper from colored construction paper. Cut most of these squares into triangles. Cut some of them into smaller triangles.

7 This is one square with a completed symmetrical design using one color, green. Other students created designs with just blue.

8 Assemble all of the squares into a composition, then tape them together on the back.

5 Place the pieces within the squares. Explore creating a variety of arrangements on the white paper. Try to make an original, unique design. It could be symmetrical where both sides are balanced or asymmetrical where the pattern is unbalanced.

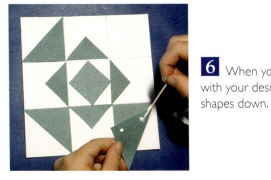

6 When you're pleased with your design, glue the shapes down.

9 This is the large paper quilt design that was created by several students. Each one designed compositions on squares using different shapes, and their combined efforts when fastened together resulted in a large, well-designed composition. Notice that the students used only blue or green on their squares which were alternated in the final quilt.

Art Activities with Paper, Clay, Fibers, and Printmaking: Using Masterworks as Inspiration

22 Crayon Batik

Grade Level
4-6

Concept
Batik is a design process originating in Southeast Asia used for coloring textiles.

Skill
Simulating the batik process with melted crayons.

Resource
Indonesian Batik

Materials
White cotton cloth; old paint brushes; wax crayons (paper removed); paraffin; muffin tin and large baking or roasting pan and hot plate, or wax melter; iron; newspapers; cold water dye and pan for dyeing; large pieces of cardboard; masking tape; rubber gloves.

Procedure
Look at the example and describe the traditional batik process. Batik is a resist-dye process where the resist substance of beeswax and paraffin is applied to the material which is dyed and the wax then removed. Mention the safety procedures for working with hot wax, iron, dye, etc.

Place a muffin tin in a large pan of water on a hot plate. Replenish the water as it evaporates. Break four or five crayons of each color into the cups, adding a one-inch cube of paraffin to each color to help the melted crayon remain fluid for a longer period. Allow the wax mixture to melt thoroughly before starting to paint. Using old brushes, one per color, have them apply wax to the cloth that is taped to a piece of cardboard to keep it smooth. For a successful batik, the wax must penetrate the cloth. After the painting is finished, check the reverse and paint over any areas that did not soak through. Lightly crumple the finished painting to crackle the waxed areas.

Place the cloth in a pan of cold water dye. Follow the timing instructions; wear rubber gloves and an apron or smock. Open the dyed painting flat on a bed of newspapers to dry. Remove the excess wax by placing the painting between sheets of clean newsprint. Apply a warm iron, using a press-and-lift motion to avoid blurring the crayon colors. The first newsprint sheets will yield an attractive monoprint. Replace the newsprint and newspapers several times until all the wax is removed and the bright batiked color remains. Display the batik paintings in the window, backlighted.

Indonesian Batik, Private Collection

Batik is a design process originating in Southeast Asia used for coloring textiles. The batik cloth you see here was created in Indonesia. Look at the organized white pattern. It was painted with wax before the fabric was dyed. The wax resisted the dye, and when it was melted and removed, the batik fabric was created. This experience will show you a design process to produce a "Crayon Batik."

1 Draw a design on a piece of paper to use as reference. Then, tape a square of cotton fabric to a piece of cardboard, and draw the design again directly on the cloth.

batik: *a process used to add color and design to paper or cloth; wax is the material utilized to protect areas from coloration by the dyes*

Fibers and Designing Activities

2 Select crayons of different colors and remove the paper. Break several pieces of each color into the cups of a wax melter. Add a small cube of paraffin to each cup and allow the mixture to melt thoroughly.

3 Using an old paintbrush, paint your design with different colors of wax. Paint the wax on heavily so it penetrates the cloth.

4 Continue painting the wax on the fabric until your design is covered. Use a different paintbrush for each color of wax. Leave some spaces unpainted around your subject. Remove the tape and look at the reverse side of the cloth. If the wax has not penetrated thoroughly, paint over those areas.

5 When the wax is dry, crumple the cloth lightly to crackle the waxed areas. This will allow the dye to penetrate the fabric and create interesting fine lines in the design.

6 Wearing rubber gloves, immerse the fabric in a container of cold water dye. When it has absorbed the dye, remove the fabric. The dye will evenly penetrate the fabric but not the areas covered with colored wax.

7 Spread the dyed painting flat on a bed of newspapers, cover the fabric with more newspapers, and press it firmly with your hands to remove as much excess dye as possible. After the fabric has dried, place a sheet of newsprint over it, and apply a warm iron using a press-and-lift motion to prevent blurring the colors.

8 The crayon wax has melted from the warm iron and sticks to the paper. Replace and iron the newsprint several times until all the wax is removed from the fabric.

9 This is the completed crayon batik. The color from the crayons remained on the design, and the dye colored only the background and the fine lines created by crackling the wax.

Art Activities with Paper, Clay, Fibers, and Printmaking: Using Masterworks as Inspiration

23 Weaving in the Round

Grade Level
5–6

Concept
Weaving can become a soft sculpture.

Skill
Making a tapestry in three dimensions.

Resource
The Hand by Magdalena Abakanowicz, fiber (mag-dah-*lay*-nah ab-uh-*kahn*-oh-witz)

Materials
Cardboard tubes; yarns; large-eyed yarn needles; scissors; masking tape; wire cutters and 20 or 24 gauge copper or brass wire; texture materials such as beads, weeds, pods, shells, bells, feathers.

Procedure
Look at the examples, analyze the materials and process, and discuss additional options.

Have the students notch, or clip, both ends of the tube with scissors, every ¼ inch for small tubes, ⅜ inch to ½ inch for oatmeal cartons. Then, they fasten one end of a smooth, strong yarn or string inside the tube with masking tape and warp the outside of the tube, catching the warp yarn in the notches and fastening the end inside the tube. Students weave up and down as well as around the tube with assorted colors and textures of yarn, skipping some warps and pulling others close together. They weave only halfway down long tubes, leaving the rest of the warp to be tied off as fringe. On short tubes, a fringe can be added by looping strands of yarn onto the bottom loops of the warp as it is removed from the "loom." The weaving is removed from the tube, and students thread a piece of wire through each loop at the top. Additional yarn is tied to the wire circle for hanging. Textural materials can be tied onto the weaving itself and also to the fringe for accents.

Magdalena Abakanowitz, Polish, born 1930. *The Hand*, 1976. Fiber sculpture. American Craft Council, Minneapolis, MN

This is a three-dimensional fiber sculpture called *The Hand* by Polish artist Magdalena Abakanowicz.

These are two woven sculptures students made. They created unusual designs by weaving varied colors and textures of fibers on a round loom. We'll explore how this is done in this activity.

1 Notch both ends of a cardboard cylinder with scissors every half-inch. Then, fasten one end of strong yarn or string inside the tube with tape and **warp** the tube by bringing the string through the notches at the top and the bottom.

Fibers and Designing Activities

warp: *the set of lengthwise yarns through which the yarn is woven*

2 Using a plastic needle with a large eye and many colors and textures of yarn, weave up and down and around the tube by bringing the yarn over one warp and under the next.

3 Change colors often for an interesting color design.

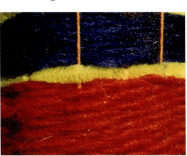

4 Weave colored chenille into the design for texture variation. Here you can see a detail of the weaving.

5 Instead of weaving completely around the tube with one color, try weaving a section of the tube with one color, tying it off, then using another color for another section.

6 The weaving is removed from the cylinder and wire strung through the loops at the top to keep the shape round. The warp at the bottom of the weaving is cut then tied.

7 Here, you can compare the weaving on the cylinder with the completed weaving. Notice that beads have been added to the warp at the bottom and yarn at the top for hanging.

Art Activities with Paper, Clay, Fibers, and Printmaking: Using Masterworks as Inspiration

24 Big Bold Banners

Grade Level
5-8

Concept
Banners and hangings are decorative devices.

Skill
Designing and fabricating a large scale banner.

Resource
Student banner

Materials
Rolls of colored paper at least 24 inches wide, butcher or craft paper, shelf paper (solid color); markers, crayons, paint and brushes; assorted colored construction and tissue papers; scissors; glue; felt or fabric scraps; yarn; dowels; straight pins.

Procedure
Show the example and talk about the variety of uses of decorative cloth and banners, including beautifying the school environment, promoting an event, celebrating a holiday. Banners and hangings have a rich and colorful history, from ancient Roman through the Crusades and medieval Europe until today, carrying symbols for secular, church, and military organizations and for pure enjoyment.

Students may work individually or with partners to design and construct large banners to decorate the halls for special occasions. Distribute newsprint and encourage drawings that feature symbols, borders, and decorative lettering. The actual banner may be made of felt or other sturdy cloth and decorated with cutouts of felt. White glue, exposed until it becomes tacky, can be used to fasten the cloth and yarn without bleeding through.

To make a paper banner, have students fold over and glue one end of a 6-foot length of 24-inch (or 8-foot length of 36-inch) paper, leaving space to insert a dowel. Using crayon and watercolor (resist technique) or markers, they draw and decorate then cut out letters for the banner. They can create decorative elements according to the theme of the banner in the same technique. They place them to create a balanced design with the cut letters, then glue everything down. Borders or decorative edges can be added. Decorate the dowel with yarn or tissue tassels after inserting it through the top border. Hang the banner with string or heavy yarn.

Student work

Large **banners** celebrating holidays, announcing an event, or simply for enjoyment and decoration have a colorful history. Banners carry decorative or meaningful symbols, shapes, and words. This is a banner showing African animals.

1 This banner was also made by students to promote a school event. Several students worked together to create it. Ideas were discussed, and each student participated in designing the elements for the banner.

2 To begin the production of a banner, first draw words, symbols, and decorations for the banner on paper. After they're cut out, they'll be used as patterns for the fabric.

3 Pin the paper letters onto the felt fabric as a pattern for accurate cutting.

Fibers and Designing Activities

4 After you have determined your arrangement of the design elements on the background of the banner, apply glue to the letters and symbols to secure them.

banner: a long strip of cloth bearing a slogan or design, hung in a public place or carried in a procession.

8 These students evaluate their banner for any final design additions.

5 Press the letters on the banner firmly.

6 Continue cutting other shapes for the banner from felt.

9 Notice how the figures on the banner were cut to show motion and emphasize the activities.

7 The tree shapes add a decorative element to the overall design. Notice the zigzag linear element representing grass under the trees.

10 The completed banner is being displayed by the teacher and two of the students who worked on the design.

53

25 Words That Do What They Say

Grade Level
6-8

Concept
"The medium is the message."

Skill
Designing letters and words that represent the meaning of the message.

Resource
Road sign and student work.

Materials
Paper at least 12 x 18 inches; pencils; crayons; felt pens; actual textured materials such as toothpicks, aluminum foil, sandpaper, cotton balls; glue; stapler; scissors.

Procedure
Explain that graphic designers, or commercial artists, often are called upon to develop letter and word shapes that carry special meanings — that "look like what they say." Look at the example and others collected from magazines, newspapers, and advertising mailers. Analyze the variations from standard letter shapes. Propose a few words to play with such as thin, tiny, striped, flexible, and solicit more from the students.

Distribute 12 x 18-inch paper and suggest that students consider changing the shape and/or dimensions to further emphasize the "personalities" of the words they select. Allow them access to a wide assortment of drawing and collage materials. Students should pre-plan on newsprint first, making thumbnail sketches and then full scale designs. Encourage originality and good craftsmanship.

Graphic designers are commercial artists who must develop letter and word shapes that carry special meanings. A graphic designer designed this road sign with the placement of letters that look like its message of a rough road ahead.

1 Look at magazines to see if you can find words that do what they say. Think about a design you could make with a word that would represent what it is or means. These examples of students' work will give you some ideas for this experience.

graphic design: a creative process which combines words, symbols, and images to create a visual representation of ideas and messages

Fibers and Designing Activities

2 Sketch several ideas, then select the best one to use as reference. Draw the final design carefully on painting paper.

6 Arrange the letters on a background paper. Can you see where the student has added bandages to further emphasize his design?

3 This student used the word "finger" and drew each letter to look like a finger. Knuckles of a finger represent the curved part of a letter. The design is then painted.

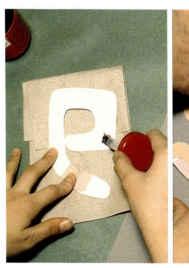

7 Now, the letters are glued to the background.

4 Use colors that are appropriate for your word.

5 After your design is painted and has dried, cut out each letter of your word.

8 This is the completed design. What word can you think of to try to design the letters to represent its meaning?

26 Coiled Baskets

Grade Level
6–8

Concept
A basket can be made from coiled, wrapped fiber.

Skill
Learning the coil technique of basketry.

Resource
Navajo Basket

Materials
4 or 5-ply jute (the kind used for patio plant hangers) or earth-colored cotton roving, ¼-inch diameter; sturdy medium to heavyweight yarn, such as acrylic rug yarn; raffia needle; scissors.

Procedure
Show the example and discuss Native American basketry. Note the craftsmanship and the designs.

With an arm's length of yarn threaded on the raffia needle, students lay the last inch or so of yarn along the tip of the jute, double it back over the end, then down to the tip again and begin wrapping it around and around to cover the last 1½ inches completely. This end is formed into a small spiral, and holding it firmly, a few stitches are taken into the center to secure it from unwinding.

The coil grows by a process of wrapping the yarn three or four times around the jute and then taking a stitch with the needle around the previous coil. This stitch can be either hidden by making a "figure eight" or decorative by taking a long stitch and bridging two coils. New yarn may be added by laying it along the uncovered jute and covering it by 4 or 5 wraps and stitches of the old yarn which is then laid along the jute and covered by wrapping and stitching with the new yarn. Sometimes a second color of yarn is carried along under the wrapping to appear at intervals, forming a design. New jute is added by splicing. Separate the strands of the old piece when about 1½ inches remain, and cut the strands to varying lengths. Do the same to the end to be joined. Overlap these tapered ends and wrap-and-stitch them as one.

To form the basket, slightly overlap each successive coil, gently pulling the flat shape up to a rounded form as the work continues. To finish the basket, taper the jute as described above, covering it with wrapping and stitching until it disappears. Run the yarn back under previous wrapping and clip it off.

Navajo basket. Private collection

This coiled basket made by Navajo people many years ago was used as a container for food. It was made by wrapping fiber rope or jute with plant fibers, then coiling it into a basket. Look at the design that was made by alternating colors.

This is a close-up of the Navajo basket which shows the coiling in detail.

1 In this activity, you will learn how to coil a basket with the same technique the Navajo used. Begin by cutting the end of a long length of rope at an angle. Lay about an inch of colored yarn on the rope, then wrap the yarn around it to cover the loose end. Bend the covered rope into a small, tight spiral. Secure the end of the rope to the length of rope by wrapping the yarn around both. Thread the loose end of yarn through a raffia needle and put a few stitches through the center of the spiral to secure it.

Fibers and Designing Activities

2 Continue wrapping the yarn around the rope, then coiling it. Every inch or so, take a stitch with the needle around the previous coil to secure it in place.

Navajo: the second largest Native American tribe of the United States of America

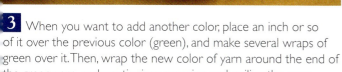

3 When you want to add another color, place an inch or so of it over the previous color (green), and make several wraps of green over it. Then, wrap the new color of yarn around the end of the green yarn, and continuing wrapping and coiling the rope.

4 Don't forget to take a stitch through a previous coil after every few wraps.

5 Change colors of yarn several times for a more interesting design. These pictures show you the process again with blue yarn.

6 To form the basket, slightly overlap each successive coil, gently pulling the flat shape up to a rounded form.

7 You can snip off the ends of yarn that were left when you changed colors.

8 To finish the basket; cut the end of the rope to taper it. Then, stitch around the end of the rope and through the previous coil, wrapping and stitching until the end disappears. Stitch through the coil several more times, then clip off the end of the yarn.

9 Compare the yarn coiled basket with the Navajo fiber coiled basket. Can you see the similar techniques?

10 Here is the completed basket. The different colors and the stitches used to secure the coils have made a good design.

57

Art Activities with Paper, Clay, Fibers, and Printmaking: Using Masterworks as Inspiration

27 Clay Owl Ornament

Grade Level
4–5

Concept
Clay is easy to form and shape.

Skill
Imprinting and folding a clay slab.

Resource
Owl by Pablo Picasso (*pah*-bloh pee-*kahs*-oh)

Materials
½–¾ lb. of terracotta clay for each student; rolling pins; very large screws or small spools, (for impressing owl's eyes); plastic spoons or forks, kitchen utensils, or broken combs (for feathers); clay cloths; tempera paint and brushes; sponges; liquid wax; leather cord for hanging, pencils.

Procedure
Show the example and discuss earlier occasions when students may have experimented with pressing objects into clay to create textures. Have students look at pictures of owls, then make a rough drawing to use as a guide. Distribute clay cloths, texture tools, and a ball of clay the size of a medium orange to each student. Supervise them as they follow the teacher demonstration one step at a time.

Pat or roll out the clay to form a long, oval shape. Smooth the edges. Write initials on the shape and turn it over. Lay a pencil across the oval about one-quarter from the top and fold the clay down over it lightly. Join the overlapped clay. Be sure the pencil can be removed easily later. With a cylindrical object (spool, screw, round-shaped object), press firmly to make two eyes. Pull out or add a beak and ears; add claws or press them in with a fork. Use either end of the fork or spoon, or another texturing tool, to impress feathers, or comb them in. Remove the pencil carefully and set the owl aside to dry for 2–3 weeks, slowly, before firing in a kiln.

After firing, the owls may be painted with clear glaze and refired. Or, "antique" them by coating with tempera, sponging off the paint from the surface, drying thoroughly, and dipping in liquid floor wax. Thread a leather cord through the passage and hang the owls in the school for decoration.

Pablo Picasso, Spanish, 1881–1973. *Owl*, 1950. Bronze, Height: 14⅜ in. Private Collection. © 2011 Estate of Pablo Picasso / Artists Rights Society (ARS), New York

This sculpture called *Owl* was made by Spanish artist Pablo Picasso. He first sculpted the form then modeled the eyes, beak, and the feathers. It was later cast into bronze.

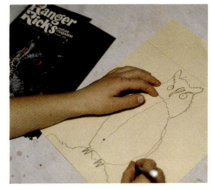

1 In this activity, you will imprint a slab of clay to look like an owl. Before you begin, look at pictures of owls and select one to use as a model for your sculpture. Sketch the image so that you will know where the eyes are, the shape of the head and body, and the texture of the feathers.

2 Roll out a piece of clay into a slab using a roller. Cut a large oval shape out of the slab. Lay a pencil across the top of the slab, and fold the clay lightly over it. This will be the top of the head. With a small cylinder, press firmly to make two eyes.

3 Cut out a beak from the excess clay, press it onto the owl, and mold it with your fingers to your desired shape.

Modeling and Constructing Activities

kiln: *a very hot oven used to bake and harden materials such as clay and bricks*

4 Use kitchen utensils or other objects to imprint the body with feather-like marks. Here, a meat tenderizer and slotted spoon are used to imprint other feather shapes on the owl.

5 Now, cut out the owl's feet from the excess clay of your slab. Attach them to the body of the owl by pressing them in firmly.

6 Look at your image and see if more feather marks are needed. The end of a fork is a good tool to use.

7 When your image is complete, remove the pencil from the top of the owl. Set the owl aside to dry, then fire it in a **kiln**. Here are two clay owl images after they have been fired.

8 Now, paint the surface of the owl with brown tempera paint.

9 Sponge off the paint with a damp sponge. Notice that some of the color will remain. Let the sculpture dry thoroughly.

10 Then, dip the owl into liquid wax. Sponge off any excess wax so that there is just an even coating on the owl.

11 Thread a leather cord through the passage in the owl's head so it can be hung for decoration.

12 Two students evaluate their completed sculptures. Notice how the imprinting gives a feathery texture to the owl's bodies.

59

Art Activities with Paper, Clay, Fibers, and Printmaking: Using Masterworks as Inspiration

28 Clay Hang Ups

Grade Level
4-6

Concept
Impressing objects in clay creates textures. Clay forms can be joined with string to make a mobile.

Skill
Imprinting moist clay to make a textured surface and joining pieces with string.

Resource
Beebop by Timothy Rose

Materials
About one pound of clay for each child; clay-cloths; drinking straws; texturing tools (found objects); tempera paints and brushes; sponges; liquid floor wax; paperclips; cord or leather thong.

Procedure
Look at the example and explain that a mobile is a construction or sculpture of shapes suspended so that it moves in a current of air. Then, demonstrate how clay can be impressed with fingers or a variety of found objects, resulting in a textured surface. Distribute clay-cloths and three pieces of clay to each child the size of a large orange, a small orange, and a lemon. Start with the smallest piece. Guide children to pat or roll the clay into a "cookie" no thinner than a child's thumb (about 3/8 inch). With a straightened paperclip, trim some edges away to make an interesting shape. Smooth the edges with a fingertip. Scratch initials on the shape and turn it over. Use a fat drinking straw to punch holes for hanging.

Have the children texture the clay by pressing it with "beautiful junk," pods, cones, bolts, screws, combs, plastic utensils, sticks. Put the first shape on a shelf and proceed to flatten, initial, trim, punch, and texture the other pieces. After the slabs have air-dried slowly for 2-3 weeks, fire them in a kiln.

The children can paint them after firing with colored tempera paint, filling all the cracks. Sponge off the paint, leaving a stain in the crevices. Let dry, then dip each piece in liquid floor wax. String groups of three into a mobile with short lengths of leather thong or cord and hang them.

Timothy Rose, *Beebop*, stainless steel/stainess steel wire. 60 inches long, 72-inch span. www.mobilesculpture.com

A mobile is a group of hanging objects that move freely. American artist Timothy Rose created this mobile called *Beebop*. Notice the different shapes and sizes of the objects which make the mobile interesting. In this activity, you'll use clay to make objects for hanging in a mobile.

1 Roll a piece of clay into a slab.

2 Select a variety of found objects to use as texturing tools for your clay shapes.

mobile: *a group of hanging objects that move freely*

Modeling and Constructing Activities

3 After the clay has been cut or formed into large and small shapes, imprint the shapes with the texturing tools. Impressing different textures in each shape will create an interesting design.

4 Punch holes in the shapes with a drinking straw so the pieces can be joined with cord. The larger shapes will need several holes.

5 Here are a variety of shapes ready to be dried and fired. These are nonobjective shapes; they do not represent any real object. The textural design makes them interesting.

6 After firing, paint the shapes with tempera paint, then sponge the paint off. After the paint dries, paint the shapes with liquid wax.

7 String the shapes together with colored cord. The largest shape should be on the top and the smallest on the bottom.

8 These mobiles were hung in the schoolyard for all the students to enjoy. Can you see the interesting designs made by imprinting textures on the shapes?

61

Art Activities with Paper, Clay, Fibers, and Printmaking: Using Masterworks as Inspiration

29 Fancy Strips

Grade Level
4-6

Concept
Paper can be manipulated into three-dimensional forms.

Skill
Paper sculpture techniques: combining curled, fringed, and folded strips.

Resource
Student work

Materials
Colored paper strips 1 x 9 inches, 1 x 12 inches (paper with a different color on each side is especially effective in this lesson); shallow boxes, or make simple containers (see below); scissors.

Procedure
Show the example of a box filled with folded, S-curved, and spiraled strips. Distribute materials to groups of 4-6 children.

Review the fan-folding technique: fold a strip in half, fourths, eighths, then unfold and refold to make a zigzag. Give children time to make a zigzag strip. Show how to roll one end of a strip tightly around a pencil, release, and roll the other end to produce either a "C" or an "S" curve. Let students experiment with this technique. Demonstrate how to fringe one end of a strip and curl or zigzag the separate small strips. Suggest that children work with the strips and fill their boxes with an array of different colors and forms of "fancy strips."

Note: To make a sample box: lay a ruler inside the edge of a 9" x 12" piece of lightweight cardboard (tagboard or shirt cardboard) and score lines from edge to edge all around with an opened scissor blade. Bend up the cardboard gently along these fold lines after clipping in from each end to make tabs. Bend the tabs around the sides and glue in place securing temporarily with paper clips or clothespins until the glue dries. Line the box with a sheet of colored paper cut to fit the bottom, if desired.

Paper can be used create three-dimensional forms. This paper sculpture shows colored strips that were folded and curled into a variety of shapes, then placed in a box. Color, line, and shape are the elements of design used in this activity.

1 These are the materials you'll use — a low box made from heavy paper or cardboard and many paper strips of different colors. These strips have contrasting colors on both sides which help create a more colorful design.

color: *visual sensation dependent on the reflection or absorption of light from a surface; hue, value, and intensity are the three main characteristics of color*

Modeling and Constructing Activities

2 To begin your sculpture, fold a paper strip to make a zigzag.

3 Curl a strip by rolling the strip tightly around a pencil.

4 These are the different shapes that can be produced by folding and curling. Can you identify the S, C, spiral, and zigzag shapes? Which make curving lines or straight lines?

5 Make many different shapes with the paper strips, then arrange them in the box. Vary the colors and shapes. Open up some of the shapes and leave some tightly curled or folded.

6 When you are satisfied with the arrangement, glue just the edge of one side of the strips to secure them to the box.

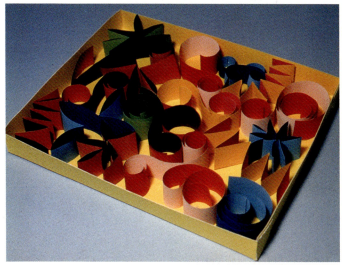

7 This is a completed paper sculpture ready to be mounted on the wall. The colors, lines, and shapes make a good design. There is rhythm in the sculpture because many of the shapes are repeated.

Art Activities with Paper, Clay, Fibers, and Printmaking: Using Masterworks as Inspiration

30 Birds, Butterflies, and Flowers

Grade Level
5-6

Concept
Two-dimensional strips of paper can be combined to make three-dimensional decorative forms.

Skill
Constructing forms from manipulated paper strips.

Resource
Student work

Materials
Paper strips, assorted colors, varying lengths but consistent width (about 1 inch); staplers or glue and paper clips.

Procedure
Look at and discuss the examples; what techniques were used (folding, curling, fringing) and how they were fastened together.

Have the students form three loops in a long paper strip and staple the ends of the loops together. They repeat this step. A long paper strip is placed between the ends of the two flowers and the three pieces stapled together. The long strip is the stem. Then, two strips are folded and stapled to the stem for the leaves. Another type of flower is made by stacking three strips and stapling or gluing an inch or two from one end. They slide the middle strip up until it bulges and the top strip until it bulges more, then they are fastened together where the fingers are holding them. Pose the problem of how three or five strips could be bulged symmetrically on both sides of the center, and demonstrate if necessary. Circulate through the class to help as the students experiment.

Encourage exploration of bird, butterfly, and flower forms and other decorative designs. Completed paper sculptures may be suspended on threads to make mobiles or touch-glued on edge to a background paper for display.

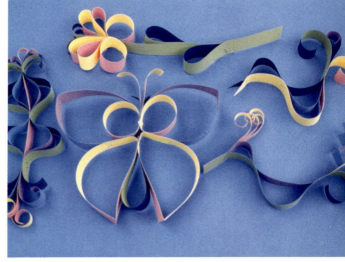

Colored strips of paper can be shaped into the **form** of a bird, butterfly, and flowers, as you can see here. We'll show you how this is done in this activity.

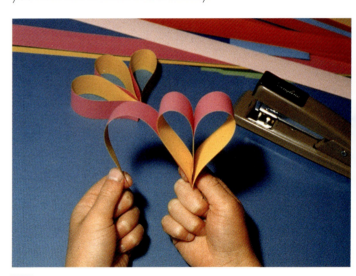

1 To make a flower, form three loops in a long paper strip.

2 Staple the ends of the loops together.

3 Make another flower. Place one long green paper strip between the ends of the two flowers and staple the three pieces together. The green strip becomes the stem.

Modeling and Constructing Activities

4 To make leaves for your flower, fold two green strips, and staple them to the stem.

5 The completed flower is ready to hang by attaching a string or could be put in a vase for decoration.

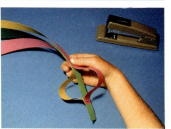

6 Another stem can be made by stacking three paper strips and stapling them about an inch from one end. Slide the outside strips down until they make a bulge on either side of the main stem and staple.

7 Make two more bulges of the same size.

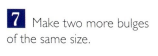

8 Add a large paper strip flower to the stem.

form: *a three-dimensional figure that may be freeform or geometric, natural or man-made.*

10 These pictures show one way to make a butterfly. Place the ends of one long strip together and staple it. With two shorter strips, form the butterfly's lower wings and staple them to the body. With longer strips, shape the upper wings and fasten them to the body. Make loops of the inner wings and staple these parts together. Additional loops could be added inside the wings.

11 Try experimenting with other shapes. Notice the bird sculpture in the top right that was made in the same way as the flowers and butterfly. See what other forms you can invent.

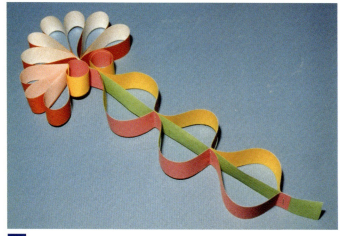

9 This is the completed flower. Can you see how the curved lines and shapes were made?

Art Activities with Paper, Clay, Fibers, and Printmaking: Using Masterworks as Inspiration

31 Dragon Puppet

Grade Level
5-8

Concept
A toy can be made from readily available materials and objects intended for other uses.

Skill
Designing and constructing a hand puppet.

Resource
Student work

Materials
White or colored adult-sized tube socks; scraps of felt; buttons, feathers, tissue, rubber bands; 3 x 5-inch index cards, scissors, glue.

Procedure
Look at the example and pictures of dragons and discuss the significant features, scarey big mouths that breathe fire, bulging eyes, feathers and scales, and paws with claws.

Demonstrate how to make the dragon puppet's mouth, eyes, and scaley mane before distributing materials to groups of five or six children. Mouth: fold an index card end-to-end and trim off the corners. Spread glue on top and bottom and clamp over the toe of a tube sock. Turn sock inside out. Eyes: make a wad of tissue paper, poke it up inside to where an eye will be and trap it in place with a small rubber band wrapped around the bump outside. Repeat for the second (and third) eye. Scales: the row of scales along the dragon's neck and back will be made from a strip of felt about 1½ x 12 inches. Cut in one inch at one-inch intervals and spread the tabs alternately left and right. Glue down the middle of the body. Put a scrap of cardboard or paper inside the sock first to avoid gluing the body together.

Talk about a variety of ways to individualize the dragons with feathers, fur, beads, bows and buttons, sequins and shiny paper, Styrofoam popcorn, pipecleaners, and old dimestore jewelry. Supervise the children and assist as they create imaginative, personalized puppets.

Extensions: Plan a play such as "A Day in Dragon School" or take a Dragon Parade to the class next door.

This student is holding a dragon puppet constructed from a tube sock. Learn how to make your own **hand puppet**.

1 Collect the materials you'll need to make your puppet: a sock, scraps of felt, some small feathers, and shiny paper. A small piece of cardboard will be needed to make the puppet's mouth.

2 Fold the cardboard in half and cut the corners. Place the fold over the toe end, and glue both sides to the sock. Then, pull the sock inside out over the cardboard.

Modeling and Constructing Activities

hand puppet: *a puppet with a cloth body and hollow head that fits over the hand*

3 This student tried on the hand puppet so she could check the construction of the mouth.

4 To make the dragon's eyes, wad a piece of tissue paper, and poke it up inside the sock. Fasten it in place with a small rubber-band wrapped around the bump outside.

5 The inside of the mouth is made from a piece of folded felt which is rounded with scissors and glued inside the mouth. Cut out a fiery tongue from a piece of felt, and glue it in the mouth. Cut circles from silver and red paper to glue to the eyes.

6 Make the scales for the dragon's neck and back from a long strip of felt. Cut slashes on one side and zigzag cuts on the other.

7 Glue the scales down the middle of the body. Decorate the dragon by gluing down feathers.

8 The completed dragon hand puppet was easily constructed. Think about other hand puppets you could make in this way.

Art Activities with Paper, Clay, Fibers, and Printmaking: Using Masterworks as Inspiration

32 Cylinder Sillies

Grade Level
5-8

Concept
Paper can be formed into a cylinder and decorated.

Skill
Paper sculpture techniques: cutting, folding, curling, fringing, piercing, and fastening.

Resource
Women and Dog by Marisol

Materials
Colored construction paper, 12 x 18 inches; varicolored scraps of paper; scissors; glue; yarn, feathers, and other treasured trash

Procedure
Discuss Marisol's sculpture and explain that it is meant to be humorous and startling. Look at the student works and talk about how they were made.

Younger children may work better on the flat 12 x 18-inch paper, in which case, draw guidelines to keep the features in the center third. Older children can staple or glue the paper into a cylinder first, then add features. This is a good opportunity to talk about formal symmetry; how the features are balanced, with the nose on the midline. Remind children how to cut symmetrical shapes on a folded paper. Distribute materials and set children to work.

As the features are cut and decorated, children may fasten them on the cylinders making sure some stick out three-dimensionally. Eyebrows and eyelashes may be fringed and curled, hair may be parted and pulled back and caught with gaudy paper ribbons or stapled behind enormous ears. Dangling earrings and bone nose ornaments may hang through pierced ears and noses. Tongues may extend through gaping or grinning mouths. Collars and ties or necklaces can encircle the cylinder necks. A variety of paper sculpture and fastening techniques should be explored by each child.

Extensions: Wrap construction paper around paper towel cores and create tall, slim, silly cylinder figures. Name the "sillies" and write verses about them.

Marisol, Venezuelan, Born 1930. *Women and Dog*, 1964. Wood, plaster, synthetic polymer, taxidermied dog head, and miscellaneous items, overall: 72 x 85 x 48 in. Whitney Museum of American Art, New York; purchase with funds from the Friends of the Whitney Museum of American Art 64.17a-g. Art © Marisol / Licensed by VAGA, New York, NY. Photograph by Robert E. Mates

Venezuelan sculptor Marisol constructs painted wood sculptures and adds plaster pieces or found objects. This one is called *Women and Dog*. The life-sized figures are meant to be humorous and startling. We'll explore constructing paper sculptures meant to be funny to look at.

1 Here are two cylinder sillies created by students. They decorated the sculptures with shapes to form the silly features.

symmetry: *a balanced proportion of parts arranged on opposite sides of a plane, a line, or a point.*

Modeling and Constructing Activities

6 Fold a piece of paper in half. Open it and draw the outline of a nose. Remember that both sides of a nose are symmetrical, or balanced. Re-fold the nose and cut it out.

7 Now, draw and cut out ears for your Cylinder Silly.

2 You'll need a piece of colored paper to form the cylinder as well as scraps of colored paper from which to cut the features.

3 Tape the large piece of colored paper into a cylinder.

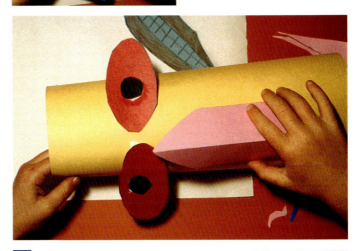

4 Draw and color a large smiling, or maybe frowning, mouth. Then, cut it out.

8 Attach the features to the cylinder. The folded nose should only be opened slightly, then glued, so it is three-dimensional. You can add other features to your sculpture. Cut fringes to make heavy eyebrows.

5 Draw, then cut out large ovals of one color and glue another color of circles to them to make eyes. Glue them to the cylinder.

9 This student is displaying her Cylinder Silly. Although the features are symmetrically placed, they are unusually large.

69

Art Activities with Paper, Clay, Fibers, and Printmaking: Using Masterworks as Inspiration

33 Helmet Mask

Grade Level
5-8

Concept
Some masks are worn over the top of the head like a helmet.

Skill
Constructing a tagboard strip helmet and decorating it.

Resource
African Bamun Helmet Mask. African Bakuba Helmet Mask.

Materials
Strips of tagboard, 1½ x 24 inches; scraps of colored construction paper and specialty papers such as mylar, metallic, or "patent-leather" paper; scissors; glue; stapler.

Procedure
Look at the examples and analyze how they were constructed and worn. Encourage students to be as imaginative as possible in this project. Demonstrate how to cut a 1½-inch strip of tagboard long enough to encircle the wearer's head just above the ears and overlap 2 inches; staple it closed; then add strips of tagboard that go over the student's head from ear to ear and from the back of the head to the front. This will make a basic helmet upon which to fasten subsequent paper shapes. Supervise children as they work in pairs to complete this step. Good craftsmanship is essential here.

Have the children slash two sheets of 12 x 18-inch colored construction paper lengthwise every ¾ inch, stopping about 2 inches from the end. They glue or staple this border around the helmet and gather all loose strips into a topknot, tie with bright ribbon, and curl the ends. This will cover the helmet structure. Then, they cut an enormous nose from folded paper, decorate it, and attach it to the center front so that it hangs to the chin. Two outrageously ornate eyes with eyebrows are added. Elongated ears can be enhanced with paper chain earrings. More strips of paper hair can be added to cover the wearer's neck and garnished with jeweled stick-ons. Show off!

Left: Helmet Mask. Africa, Equatorial Africa, Cameroon grasslands, Bamum people, early 20th Century, c. 1900. Wood; Height 57.2 cm. © The Cleveland Museum of Art. Gift of Mr. and Mrs. William D. Wixom in memory of Mr. and Mrs. Ralph M. Coe 1967.151. Right: Helmet Mask (Bwoom). Central Africa, Democratic Republic of the Congo, Kuba people, mid-late 19th century, mid-late 1800s. Wood and pigment; 43.3 x 31.2 x 28.3 cm. © The Cleveland Museum of Art., James Albert Ford Memorial Fund 1935.304

Some masks are worn over the top of the head, like a helmet. African tribes constructed **helmet masks** like the ones seen here to wear in ceremonial dances or even in warfare. The masks usually had grotesque or humorous features.

1 Here are helmet masks that children made from paper strips and scraps. In this experience, you'll learn how to make a helmet mask of your own design.

helmet mask: a mask that is worn over the top of the head like a helmet for rituals, celebrations, and protection

Modeling and Constructing Activities

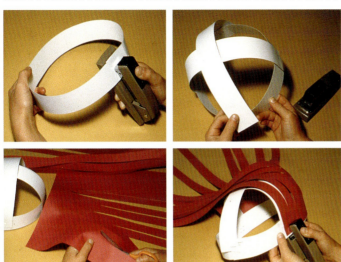

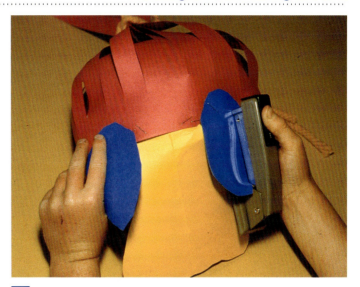

2 Measure a strip of thin cardboard to fit around your head and staple it. Staple two other strips of cardboard to the head band to make a helmet shape. Cut long slashes in a large, colorful piece of paper and staple it to the helmet.

6 Staple the nose and the eyes to the helmet.

3 Gather all the loose strips into a topknot and tie it with a colorful piece of yarn.

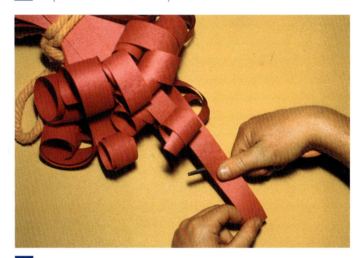

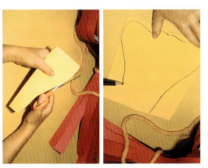

4 Draw and cut out an enormous nose. Remember that to have both sides of the nose symmetrical, fold the paper before cutting it.

7 Now, curl the hair by running a scissors down the paper strip to the end. Curl all the strips.

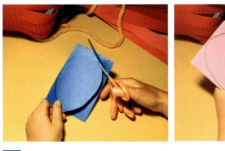

5 Cut out huge eyes and ears.

Helmet Mask. © The Cleveland Museum of Art. Gift of Mr. and Mrs. William D. Wixom in memory of Mr. and Mrs. Ralph M. Coe 1967.151.

8 A student wears the helmet mask she constructed. Compare it to the African helmet mask shown on the right. How are they alike and how are they different?

Art Activities with Paper, Clay, Fibers, and Printmaking: Using Masterworks as Inspiration

34 Cutting a Figure

Grade Level
4-5

Concept
The proportion of the human figure.

Skill
Assemble parts to form a human figure.

Resource
Both Members of this Club by George Bellows

Materials
9 x 12-inch paper or tagboard and one piece 3 x 4½ inches for each child; scissors, glue, or ⅜-inch paper fasteners; chalk or charcoal; crayons or tempera paint; scraps of patterned paper or cloth.

Procedure
Look at Bellows' painting and point out that before he could create this painting, he studied how the human body looked and moved. Use an artist's mannequin as a reference. Talk about the proportions of the human figure. How wide is the head in relation to the shoulders? How long are the arms in relation to the legs? Where do the arms bend, in relation to the waist? Where do fingertips meet the thighs? How many heads tall is a child; an adult?

Show an enlarged representation of the 9 x 12-inch paper and indicate where it will be folded and cut to make four 6 x 4½-inch pieces. Distribute the materials and supervise students as they work: 1) Fold one piece of 6 x 4½-inch paper in half lengthwise and draw a long oval, filling the space (the upper legs). 2) Fold the same for the lower legs but include the ankles and feet in the length. 3) Fold the third piece into fourths, crosswise, to make sections 4½ x 1½ inches; draw two ovals filling the spaces and two smaller ones with wrists and hands included. 4) Make a pear-shaped body, using the full length and most of the width of the last 6 x 4½-inch piece. 5) On the 3 x 4½-inch piece, draw a head and neck, filling the space.

Check to see that the drawings have been made full-size. Have students cut out the shapes, then assemble the pieces in ways to indicate action, overlapping the shapes slightly. Touch-glue or punch holes and join with paper fasteners. The students can complete the figures by coloring with crayons or paints and/or by collaging bits of paper or fabric for clothing.

George Bellows, American, 1882–1925. *Both Members of This Club*, 1909. Oil on canvas, 45¼ x 63 3/16 in. (115 x 160.5 cm). National Gallery of Art, Washington, DC, Chester Dale Collection. 1944.13.1.

This painting is called *Both Members of This Club* by American artist George Bellows. Before he could paint this action scene, he studied how the human body looked and moved. This understanding assists an artist in accurate portrayals of figures.

1 Do you know the proportions of the human figure and the relationship of one part to another? Look at your own body and other students to study the proportions of the head, arms, and legs to the body. A **mannequin** is also a helpful reference for artists.

2 To begin, fold a piece of manila paper into four sections. Cut the sections apart. You will also need a smaller rectangle for a head.

Modeling and Constructing Activities

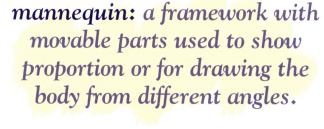

mannequin: *a framework with movable parts used to show proportion or for drawing the body from different angles.*

 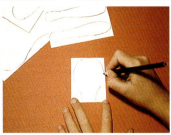

2 On one section of paper, draw the approximate shape of a body. On another piece, draw long shapes of the upper arms and lower arms separately. Draw the upper legs or thighs on a single section of paper. Draw the lower legs and feet on the last section. On the small rectangle, draw the shape of a head.

5 You can see the body beginning to take shape here.

3 Now, cut out all of the pieces of the body.

6 The completed paper figure is posed in a position of action. Try moving each part of the figure into other positions. Does it move very much like your own body?

4 Punch holes in the body, head, arms, and legs so they can be fastened. Join each part of the body with paper fasteners.

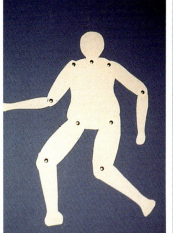 

7 Both the paper figure and the mannequin look like they are running. You can use the paper figure as a reference for your artwork.

35 Slab Animals

Grade Level
4-6

Concept
Clay slabs can be rolled, cut, textured, and formed.

Skill
Creating abstract forms of clay.

Resource
Student work

Materials
One pound of ceramic clay for each student; clay-cloths; rolling pins or 2-inch dowels; 3/8 x 12-inch wooden sticks; texturing tools; paper clips; 4½ x 6-inch paper; newspapers; masking tape.

Procedure
Look at the example and talk about the symmetrical, flattened, "steam-rollered" characters that appear in some animated cartoons. Decide on an animal, wild, domestic, prehistoric, or imaginary, that has a distinctive form and texture. Fold the 4½ x 6-inch paper and draw half the figure on the fold. Take care to draw only half a head. Keep the outline simple and allow no part to be narrower than ½-inch; legs should be sturdy. Cut out the animal, open the paper, and when students understand the process, let them develop their individual patterns.

Demonstrate how to roll out the clay between the thickness-control slats on the clay-cloth (fabric-backed wallpaper sample). Lay the pattern on the clay and cut it out with a straightened paperclip. Smooth the edges after removing the excess clay. Supervise students as they complete these steps. Demonstrate on some of the scrap clay how to make a variety of textures with found objects. Impress textural details but be careful not to push too hard. "Comb" a hairy coat, make scales with a craft stick or paperclip. Drape the animal over a rolled, taped newspaper. Prop up the head and tail with wads of paper and arrange the legs. Let students complete their animals.

Cover the sculptures with plastic bags or wet paper towels to retard drying. Let dry 2-3 weeks before firing and finishing with tempera paint and wax or glazing and refiring.

Here are three clay animals that have been constructed from a clay slab. Notice that they stand freely. Can you see the **texture** on their bodies? You will learn how simply a three-dimensional clay animal can be constructed.

1 Fold a piece of paper in half. This will be used for drawing a pattern for your clay slab. Now, draw only a side of an animal on the folded paper. The top of the animal should be on the fold. The animal could be realistic or imaginary. Keep the outline simple.

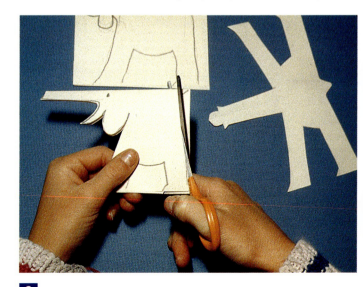

2 Cut out the animal and open the paper. The opened drawing will be your pattern for the clay slab.

Modeling and Constructing Activities

3 Roll out a piece of clay into a slab.

4 Place the paper pattern on the slab. Trace the outline with an opened paper clip. Press firmly to cut through the clay.

5 Then, remove the pattern.

7 Now, imprint a variety of textures on the clay body using found objects. Make scales with a paper clip. Comb a hairy coat with a large-toothed comb. Try using other objects to imprint textures.

8 Carefully bend the clay animal into a standing position. Adjust heads, horns, or trunks into the position you want them to have. After the animal has dried, paint it with bright colors.

6 Remove the excess clay carefully, then smooth the edges of the outline with your fingers.

texture: *the surface quality, both simulated and actual, of artwork*

9 Here are four clay animals students constructed. The three-dimensional forms stand freely. Can you see the texture on the bodies?

36 Origami Boxes

Grade Level
4-6

Concept
Paper can be folded into a functional form.

Skill
Accurate folding to make a box form.

Resource
Student work

Materials
Squares of paper 9 x 9 and 8¾ x 8¾ inches; scissors.

Procedure
Look at the example and comment that origami boxes require no glue but much attention to directions and careful folding. After students have learned the process, they may make additional boxes with papers they have decorated, such as vegetable prints or crayon resist patterns. Or they may apply cut shapes, perhaps seasonal motifs, to the completed box covers. Precut the squares accurately; each box and cover requires one piece of each size.

Fold the smaller square, 8¾ inches, diagonally; open, and fold the other diagonal; open. Bring each corner, one at a time, to the center of the square and crease the folds; open. Bring each corner, one at a time, to the middle of the fold beyond the center and crease the folds; open. Bring each corner, one at a time, just slightly forward to the closest fold; crease; open. Working on two opposite corners only, cut along the fold lines on both sides of the corner the distance of two small squares. Be sure to stop one line before the central diagonal. These corners will now look like "little houses." Bring each of these two points to the center and bend up the doubled paper forming the opposite walls of the box and reversing the folds nearest the corners, then lay them flat again. Bring the other two corners to the center the same way, thus forming the third and fourth walls. Bend the "wings" at right angles. Hold them in place temporarily with paperclips, if necessary. Bring the first corners up, over, and down to the center, locking in the wings and completing the box.

Repeat all steps with the slightly larger paper to make the cover. Decorate as desired.

Extensions: Students can make successively smaller boxes that nest inside each other.

These boxes have been constructed from paper, without glue, tape, or staples. Each box has a decorated cover. You'll learn a simple method of constructing an **origami** box in this activity.

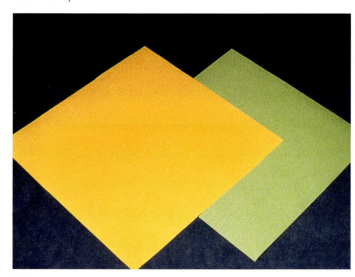

1 You'll need two square pieces of paper, one a little larger than the other. The larger piece will become the cover for the box.

origami: the Japanese art of folding paper into decorative shapes and figures

Modeling and Constructing Activities

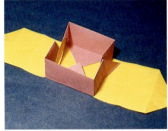

2 Fold the larger piece of paper into a triangle by meeting two corners. Press the fold firmly. Open the paper and repeat with the opposite corners.

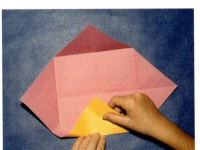

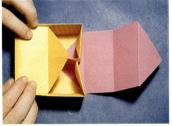

3 Open the paper and fold each corner up to the center point.

7 Turn the paper over. To make the box, bring up the point of a corner to the center fold, bend up the doubled paper, and reverse the folds nearest the corners. Follow the same procedure for the other sides as shown in these pictures.

4 Open the paper and fold each corner up to the first fold of the opposite corner.

8 Here is a completed box cover. Now, use the smaller sheet of paper to make a box that will fit inside the box cover.

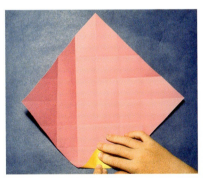

5 Then, with the paper open, fold each corner just up to its own first fold.

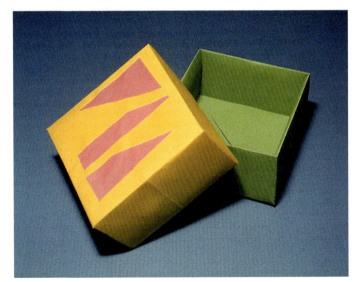

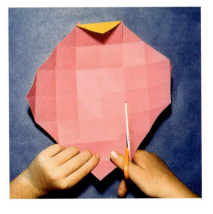

6 Cut along the fold lines the distance of two small squares on both sides of two opposite corners. Be sure you've stopped one line before the middle fold.

9 You can see here that paper can be folded into a functional form. The cover has been decorated with shapes of a contrasting color. You could put small treasures in the box for your own use or put a present in one for a friend.

77

Art Activities with Paper, Clay, Fibers, and Printmaking: Using Masterworks as Inspiration

37 A Mosaic Mask

Grade Level
5-6

Concept
Masks can be formed over the face and decorated with a paper mosaic

Skill
Modeling foil and creating a paper mosaic

Resource
Aztec Mask, Private Collection

Materials
Heavy-duty aluminum foil; newspapers; masking tape; wallpaper paste; black tempera paint; black acrylic paint; brushes; clear, glossy polymer acrylic; magazines with colored pages; scissors; white glue.

Procedure
Discuss the examples and point out that masks for rituals and ceremonies are made with care using special, often costly, materials. The Aztec people, for example, buried their dead leaders with masks made with turquoise and coral. Students will simulate real mosaic stones with paper on their masks.

Students will tear a strip of aluminum foil long enough to fold double and fit generously over their face. They should crumple it lightly and form it gently over the face, exaggerating the nose. Turn the foil under all around to make a neat edge and reinforce the mask. Then, it should be painted with black acrylic paint. Study pictures of Mexican mosaic masks and note the variations of colors in the pieces of stone. Find a variety of blue, turquoise, and jade pages in discarded magazines, and cut the colors into strips about ½-¾-in. wide. Use a toothpick to apply a spot of glue to each small mosaic piece as it is cut from a strip leaving tiny spaces between each one. Work in rows around the facial features, then fill in the rest of the surface with more pieces of varying colors. When all of the pieces have been glued on, coat the mask with clear, glossy acrylic polymer, sealing down all loose corners.

Extension: A papier maché mask can be made by placing the foil mask over a taped-down wad of newspaper to help preserve the form as pieces of newspaper dipped in wallpaper paste are applied. Torn 2 x 2-in. pieces are dipped into the paste, pulled through two fingers to remove excess, and overlapped to make a thin layer. More pieces should be added until an even coverage of four to five layers is achieved. To insure easy removal from the foil form, the first layer should be applied with water only, not paste. Before the papier maché dries completely, remove it from the form, trim, and cut out any desired openings, like the eyes or mouth. Let the mask dry thoroughly before painting it all over with black acrylic or tempera paint followed with a finish of clear acrylic polymer. The mask can then be decorated with the mosaic pieces in the same manner as the foil mask.

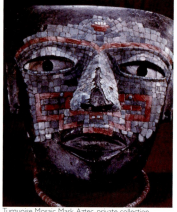 

Turquoise Mosaic Mask, Aztec, private collection.   Student work

Masks for rituals and ceremonies were often made by inlaying small pieces of precious stones with great care. Such a mask is the *Turquoise Mosaic Mask* made by Aztec Indians seen on the left. Using the same technique with small squares of colored papers, a student made the mask shown on the right. You'll learn how to make a **mosaic** mask also in this activity.

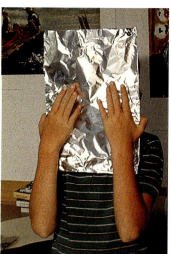 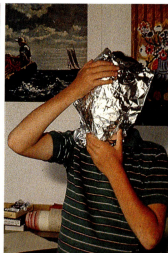

1 Double a piece of heavy aluminum foil large enough to cover your face. Crumple it lightly and form it gently to the shape of your face.

2 Turn over the edges of the foil to make a neat outline.

Modeling and Constructing Activities

3 Place the mask on crumpled newspaper to preserve the form, then paint the entire mask with black acrylic paint.

4 Select brightly colored pictures from magazines and cut out small squares for the mosaic pieces. Here different shades of green and blue resembling turquoise were selected.

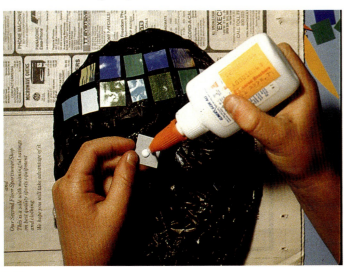

5 Glue the squares in rows across the mask, leaving tiny spaces between them.

mosaic: art consisting of a design made of small pieces of colored stone or glass

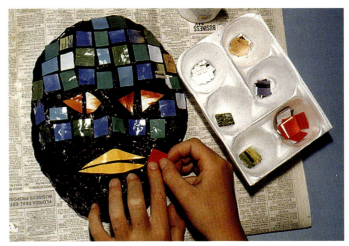

6 Cover the entire mask with squares. Eyes and a mouth should be cut from the pictures and glued to the mask, also.

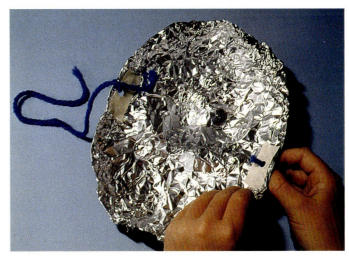

7 Place a piece of tape on the inside of the mask on both sides. Punch holes, then insert cord so the mask can be worn.

8 This is the completed mosaic mask. Can you see how the tiny squares of colored pictures resemble inlaid precious stones?

79

Art Activities with Paper, Clay, Fibers, and Printmaking: Using Masterworks as Inspiration

38 Piñata Party

Grade Level
5-8

Concept
A cultural container that is meant to be destroyed.

Skill
Assembling cardboard parts and decorating with tissue paper.

Resource
Mexican Piñata (pin-*yaht*-ah)

Materials
Scratchpaper for planning; cardboard boxes about 12 x 8 x 8 inches; lightweight cardboard; cardboard tubes; mat knife; masking tape; tissue paper (variety of colors); scissors; glue; string.

Procedure
Show the example and acquaint students with the tradition of piñatas. In Mexico, they are filled with toys or candy, hung so they can be raised and lowered, and blindfolded children take turns trying to break them open with a stick.

Each student should make a sketch plan, referring to the box shape that will hold the candy and toys. Cut a trapdoor out in the bottom. Smaller boxes, tubes, or cones can be attached with masking tape to build the desired form, traditionally animals, birds, flowers, stars.

Have students layer 5 or 6 sheets of tissue and cut them into 4-inch strips, then fold them lengthwise and slash the fold at half-inch intervals. Reverse one strip at a time to make it puff out in loops, and beginning at the outer end of an extension, glue it around in a neat row. Clip off the excess. Have students make successive rows, overlapping the glued sections of previous rows, like shingling a roof. All of the extending parts should be covered before covering the box itself. Leave the "trapdoor" uncovered. Open the pinata, reach inside, and make two small punctures opposite the door to tie a string for hanging the pinata. The piñata should be stuffed with toys and candy, the opening taped closed with tape so that it will burst with a solid hit. Then, this last section should be covered with more tissue loops. Plan a piñata party!

Note: To make a cone, roll a triangular section of a circle and tape or glue the overlapping sides. Cut slashes around the base and fold out tabs by which to fasten the cone to the basic form.

This is a piñata made in Mexico. Piñatas are usually made in the shape of an animal. A Mexican tradition is to fill a piñata with toys and candy and hang them so that blindfolded children can take turns breaking them open with a stick.

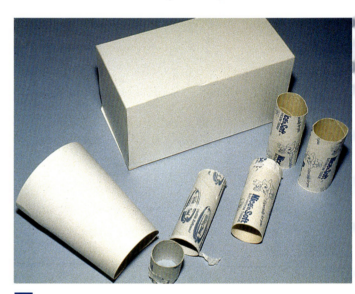

1 In this activity, you'll need the materials seen here to construct a piñata of your own design. They are a box, paper cylinders to make the legs and neck, and a piece of cardboard shaped into a cone.

2 The box is a container for the toys and candy and the cover should be closed and lightly taped while you add the decorations. It will be filled later.

Modeling and Constructing Activities

piñata: *decorated container filled with toys and candy; suspended for blindfolded children to break with sticks*

3 Cut brightly colored tissue paper into four-inch strips. Fold them in half lengthwise. Cut slashes in the fold every half-inch.

4 Reverse the fold on each strip to make it puff out in loops. Then apply glue to the uncut edges. Press the two edges together neatly.

5 Glue the strips one at a time to the top and sides of the box. Don't cover the lid of the box which is at the bottom so that it can be opened.

6 Cover the small cylinder with a strip of the looped tissue paper. Glue it to the front of the body for a neck.

7 Cover the cardboard cone for the head with strips of the tissue paper and glue the large end of it to the neck.

8 Glue tissue paper strips to the four cylinders to make the legs. Glue them to the corners of the box cover on the bottom.

9 This is the completed piñata. Wire has been attached to the body for hanging. The box can now be filled with toys and candy. With the opening lightly taped, the cover will burst open with a solid hit and students can enjoy the gifts from the piñata.

Art Activities with Paper, Clay, Fibers, and Printmaking: Using Masterworks as Inspiration

39 Model: Interior of a Room

Grade Level
5-8

Concept
Interior designers develop floor plans and wall elevations.

Skill
Making a cardboard cube and drawing a floor plan and elevations of a room.

Resource
Interior model of a building, Harry Teague

Materials
Heavy, white construction paper, at least 12 x 18 inches; pencils; felt pens; rulers; tape or glue; scissors; watercolors; brushes.

Procedure
Show the example and discuss the career of interior design as a complement to architecture and industrial design. Suggest that students think of a floor plan as a "map" of a room or building and the elevation as a plan for a vertical plane such as a wall. Students will design the floor plan and elevations for their own personal room after constructing the cube form.

Demonstrate how to draw, cut, score, and fold a cube from six attached squares. Designate one square as the floor and locate the four elevations (walls) and the ceiling of the interior of the cube. Each student will construct a cube of 4-inch squares, fold and unfold it, determine the furniture forms that the model will contain, and draw them in outline in pencil on each square. Students should refold the cube occasionally to see that the baseline of each elevation corresponds with the floor plan. After the drawing has been painted with watercolors, the model may be taped together like a box with the ceiling left unfastened. Or, students may wish to plan tabs for gluing before cutting out the cube. Some may wish to elaborate on the idea by cutting out windows and doors, by designing a larger model or a rectangular room; creating miniature 3-D furniture; or designing exterior elevations.

Extensions: Make a model to represent a room for someone living in another time or place; find out what furnishings would be appropriate.

Harry Teague, American. Interior Model of a Building.

This is a **model** of a building designed by architect Harry Teague. The top of the model has been removed so that you can see how the interior has been designed with a floor plan for a retail store.

Harry Teague, American. Interior Model of a Building.

In this close-up, you can see how the spaces were planned. Then, an interior designer develops a floor plan and selects furnishings, floor and wall coverings, and lighting fixtures.

1 In this activity, you will plan the interior of a room including doors, windows, and furniture. Look at magazine pictures of room interiors to begin planning your room. Then, draw a rough sketch of the four walls, floor, and ceiling. Draw in the furniture you want placed in the room. Then, on a large piece of cardboard, draw a grid of twelve squares.

Modeling and Constructing Activities

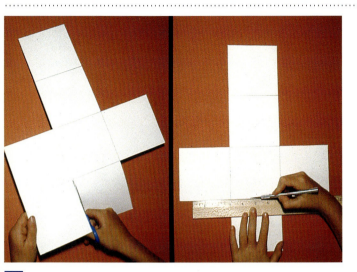

2 Cut squares from the cardboard to make a cross. Score the cardboard on the remaining lines so that the walls can be folded.

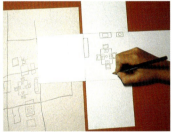

3 You can see how the walls of the model can be folded up. Now draw furniture on the floor section of the cardboard.

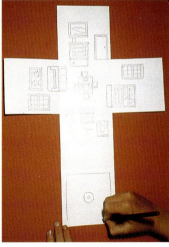

4 Draw windows, doors, light fixtures, and furniture on the four walls and ceiling.

model: representation of a proposed structure to communicate design ideas to clients and the public

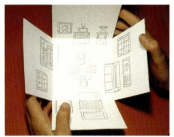

5 Check to see if your plans are accurate by folding up the walls of the model. Now, paint your drawing with watercolors. Use colors that you would like to see in a room. Begin with the floor.

6 Paint the walls including furniture, pictures, windows, and door. Fold up the walls of your interior to join the corners. Now, tape the outside corners of the walls. Your model is beginning to take shape. Can you see how the floor plan relates to the walls?

7 This is how your interior will look when it is completed. Interior designers often construct models like these to show their clients their floor plan ideas.

Art Activities with Paper, Clay, Fibers, and Printmaking: Using Masterworks as Inspiration

40 Portrait on a Pole

Grade Level
5-8

Concept
Sculptors work with armatures.

Skill
Modeling a clay head on an armature.

Resource
Alexandre Brongniart by Jean-Antoine Houdon, (al-ex-*ahnd*-reh *broh*-nyee-are; zjahn an-*twahn* oo-*don*)

Materials
For each student: 6-inch length of 1-inch dowel; 6 x 6 x 1-inch wooden base; 5 pounds terra-cotta clay; slip; paper bag; torn newspapers; masking tape; thin wire and/or sharp knife.

Procedure
Look at Houdon's sculpture and ask students to explore their own heads and faces with eyes closed, using only the tactile/kinetic clues of touch. Construct armatures by nailing a 6-inch length of 1-inch dowel to the 6 x 6 x 1-inch stand for each student sculptor. Dimensions can be enlarged if life-sized portraits are planned. Stuff a paper bag with crumpled pieces of tissue or newspaper. Invert the armature and work the dowel down to the center bottom of the bag. Gather the neck of the bag and tie or tape it firmly to the dowel where it joins the stand. Squeeze the neck area to a smaller circumference than the head and tape it firmly for better proportions later.

Each head will require several pounds of clay in ¾-1-inch slabs. Students roll out these slabs, drape them over the bag, overlap and smooth until they have an approximate thickness of ¾ inch. Check that the "skull" is shaped so as to allow adequate space for "brains." While the clay is still moist and malleable, students add protrusions such as nose and chin, ears and hair, joining securely by blending. Fingers and other tools are used to indent eye sockets, model eyes, cheeks, and forehead, until a realistic appearance is developed. If work must be extended over several days, wrap the sculpture in damp paper towels and store in airtight plastic bags between work periods. Cut the head away from the base with a taut, thin wire, but leave it on the pole. Let the head dry slowly for 4-5 weeks. Remove it gently from the pole and remove the paper. Be sure it is completely dry before bisque-firing and finishing.

Jean-Antoine Houdon, French, 1741-1828. *Alexandre Brongniart*, 1777. Marble, 15⅜ x 11¼ x 7⅜ in. (39.2 x 28.7 x 19 cm). Widener Collection, 1942.9.123. Image courtesy National Gallery of Art, Washington

1 Many artists use an **armature** on which to model the heads of their subjects. An armature will support the clay while it is being modeled. A dowel rod secured in a base makes a good armature. You'll also need a paper bag stuffed with crushed paper to place over the armature.

2 After the bag has been stuffed with paper, place it over the armature with the top of the bag touching the top of the dowel rod. Then, tie the bag at the bottom of the rod.

This is a sculpture of a head called *Alexandre Brongniart* by Jean-Antoine Houdon. Sculptures of heads are really portraits of people in a three-dimensional form. Sculptors have studied the features and contours of the head they have chosen as a subject. Close your eyes and explore the features of your head and face with your fingers. You'll work with clay in this activity to sculpt a head.

Modeling and Constructing Activities

armature: **a framework on which a sculpture is molded with clay or similar material**

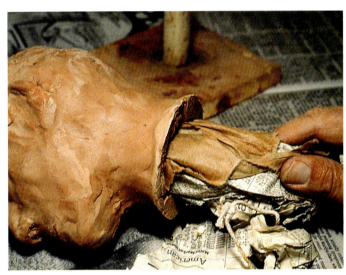

3 Place sections of clay on the form joining them with your fingers.

4 Model the features of the head. Look at your subject often or feel the contours of your own face for an accurate reproduction.

6 After the finished sculpture has dried, remove the paper from the interior.

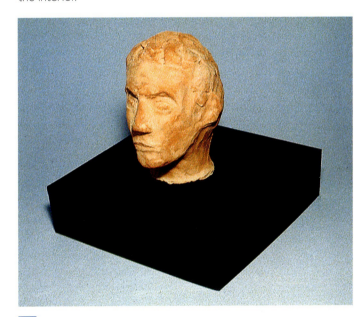

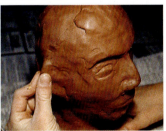 

5 You will have to add pieces of clay for some of the features and the hair. Use a wood craft stick for modeling details of features such as the nose, eyes, and ears.

7 This is the completed sculpture mounted on a base. Is the head realistically formed? Look at the details that were made with the modeling tools. Look again at sculptures by artists to see how they modeled the features and compare your work to theirs.

85

Art Activities with Paper, Clay, Fibers, and Printmaking: Using Masterworks as Inspiration

41 Clay & Gadget Prints

Grade Level
4-8

Concept
Multiple prints can be made from printing plates.

Skill
Creating a stamp design in clay and printing it. Printing with found objects.

Resource
Cylinder Seal from Cappadocia

Materials
Nonhardening clay such as plasticene; objects for impressing, found objects such as pencils, spools, bottlecaps, jar rings, potato mashers, forks, screws; tempera paint on dampened sponges or paper towel pads in low containers, one per color; large newsprint; newspapers.

Procedure
Look at the examples and discuss regular and irregular patterns and objects used to print.

Distribute the clay in lemon-sized pieces and let students explore squeezing, kneading, flattening, and impressing it. Guide them to making a ball, flattening it by stamping against the table, and pinching up a handle for it. Show the children how to impress and remove objects to change the surface. Demonstrate how to press this surface into the paint pad and stamp it onto paper four or five times, noting how each image is lighter than the previous one. Then, make a second set of prints, renewing the paint on the stamp before each print is made and compare. Distribute a different color of paint to each group of three or four students and let them experiment with regular or random prints. To vary colors, students may move to other tables, or they may trade stamps to create more interesting patterns. Wash the paint off the plasticene and let it dry before squeezing it back into balls to use another day.

Have students select from an array of found objects and explore the printing possibilities of each. After initial experimentation, suggest they choose two or three with which to print an alternating pattern. Then, have them print in the same way they printed with the plasticene stamp. Evaluate the papers in terms of organization of the motifs and craftsmanship.

Cylinder seal and imprint, period of the Assyrian merchant settlements in Cappadocia, 19th-17th BCE. Louvre, Paris, France. Photo Credit Erich Lessing / Art Resource, NY

People have been making prints for thousands of years. This is an Assyrian cylinder seal. A design was carved on the cylinder you see on the left. When the cylinder was rolled over a piece of clay, impressions or prints of the design were repeated on the surface. This is one way of relief printing.

1 To make a stamp, take a piece of clay and roll it into a ball. Then, stamp the ball on a table to flatten it. Now, press the flat side of the ball over a pencil to imprint its shape in the plasticene.

2 Turn the stamp and press the plasticene firmly over the pencil again to get the impression of a cross.

relief: *carving a surface in such a way that all that remains of the original surface is the design to be printed*

Printmaking Activities

3 Press the stamp into ink. Then, press the inked stamp on a piece of paper.

4 The stamp must be inked before each printing to make a good print. Print a random pattern. A random pattern is one that is not in organized rows.

5 Then, print an organized pattern. An organized pattern is where the shapes are repeated in the same way. Another stamp can be made by pressing just the end of a pencil all around the flat side of a plasticene stamp. You can see this design in the blue ink.

6 Here are four prints made with plasticene stamps. Can you tell which patterns are organized and which are random? Now you know how to make many prints from one printing stamp.

7 Gadgets or found objects can also be used for printing repeated patterns. You can print with such objects as a potato masher, a plastic fork, bottle caps, a cork, and the edges of foam-core pieces.

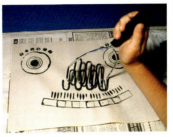 

8 An inked potato masher prints a nose on a face. A large bottle cap can be used here to print the outline of an eye.

 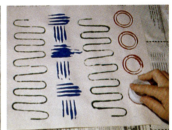

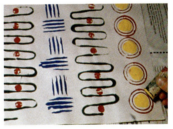

9 Make a print by printing repeated patterns with a potato masher. Use a fork to add another pattern. The bottle cap adds a different pattern. And the end of a cork adds a new color.

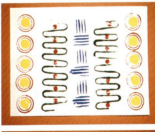 

10 Here are four completed prints made with plasticene stamps and found objects. Notice that regular and random patterns can be made by repeating the stamps.

Art Activities with Paper, Clay, Fibers, and Printmaking: Using Masterworks as Inspiration

42 Fingerpaint Monoprints

Grade Level
4-8

Concept
A monoprint is a one-of-a-kind print.

Skill
Planographic monoprinting with fingerpaint.

Resource
Anne's Roses by Sandra Kaplan

Materials
Fingerpainting paper, glossy butcher paper; fingerpaints or several colors of tempera paint and liquid starch; sponges; masking tape; newspaper; old towels for cleanup.

Procedure
Before the activity, prepare the work station. Designate one or more painting areas for the paper or if a formica surface is to be used, outline rectangles with masking tape. Place a stack of printing paper to the left, fingerpaint or the liquid starch bottle and powdered tempera paint can above it, and water and towels down the table.

Look at the example and describe the process of monoprinting. If liquid starch is used, shake a tablespoonful of powdered tempera onto the starch for the student to work into the starch and create a smooth layer of fingerpaint before beginning the design. Palms, fists, knuckles, fingertips, and fingernails should be used to vary the lines and shapes. When the picture is ready, the student carefully lays a clean paper on top of the "plate" and presses it down gently all over. The student may then peel off the monoprint and lay it aside to dry. A second, lighter print can be made next. More fingerpaint or starch and color will need to be added for each new monoprint.

1) Try different kinds of printing papers. Shiny and toothed surfaces yield different results. 2) Spread one color across the top and another over the bottom half of the "plate;" note the blended color in the middle. 3) Cut out simple paper shapes, fish, birds, leaves, and lay them on the fingerpainting before placing the monoprint paper. The print will show these as blank spaces to be drawn into with felt markers or crayons when the paint is dry.

Sandra Kaplan, American. *Anne's Roses*, 1986. Monoprint, 31 × 44 inches. © 1986 Sandra Kaplan

A monoprint is a one-of-a-kind print. American artist Sandra Kaplan painted on a piece of plastic to make this **monoprint** called *Anne's Roses*. Now, you'll learn the process of making a monoprint of your own design.

1 For this activity, you'll use fingerpaint and smear it completely over a piece of paper. This paper will be the printing plate.

monoprint: *a one-off print created when paper is pressed down on a surface that has been decorated with printing ink or painted*

Printmaking Activities

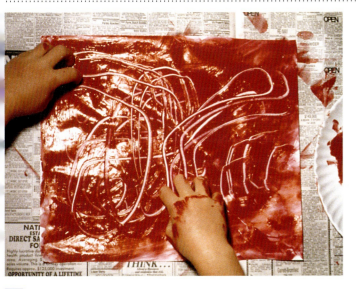

2 Use your palms, fists, knuckles, and fingernails to make a design in the wet paint. Vary the lines and shapes that you make.

5 You can now pull the print from the plate.

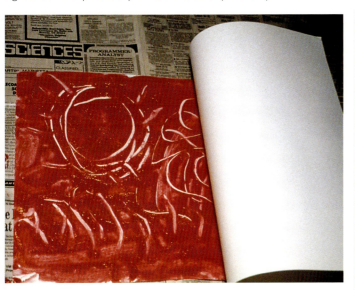

3 Place a clean piece of paper over the painted plate.

6 This is a completed monoprint. Where finger and nail marks removed the paint, the print is white.

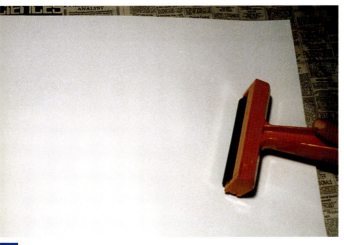

4 Then, a brayer is rolled over the paper.

43 Chalk Stencils

Grade Level
4-8

Concept
Stencils are block-outs for making the boundaries of shapes.

Skill
Preparing a simple stencil and printing from it.

Resource
Comedy, William Kanak

Materials
Poster board of heavy paper strips approximately 4 x 18 inches; manila or pale-colored construction paper 9 x 12 or 12 x 18 inches; scissors; colored chalk; facial tissues or cotton balls; fixative spray.

Procedure
Look at the example and explain that sealskin prints are made by Eskimos who cut a stencil in a seal-skin, lay it on paper, and brush ink onto the paper through the stencil. Discuss pueblo architecture noting rooflines, doors, ladders, and earth colors.

Show how to cut a tagboard strip to make the pueblo stencil by drawing an unbroken line (see illustration). Separate the parts. Have students make their own stencils, then chalk the edge of the lower section with blue and turquoise to represent the color of a sky and place it about one-third down from the top of the drawing paper; or lay the stencil on the paper first, then chalk the edge. Holding the stencil firmly, they brush the chalk up onto the paper with tissue or cotton. They then chalk the upper part of the stencil with brown and tan, placing it along the skyline and brushing the color down to tone the highest row of the pueblo homes. Students should vary the stencil and the color mix for two or three more rows of buildings. Add figures and details such as doors, windows, and ladders to connect the "apartments" of the pueblo. Encourage students to explore combinations of earth and sky colors and to use various sections of their stencils. Spray the finished pictures with fixative.

Extensions: Cut stencils with gentle curves and use them with blue and violet chalks to make faraway mountain ranges; draw or paint a blossoming tree in the foreground in the manner of a Chinese scroll. Or, use the curved stencils to make waves on which to draw a boat or an underwater picture of sea life.

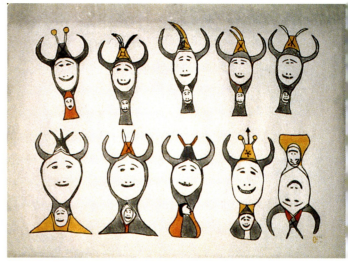

A **stencil** is used to block out shapes that artists do not wish to print. This is a stencil print on seal skin called *Comedy* by an Inuit artist, William Kanak.

1 This is a chalk stencil print a child made of Indian pueblos. Let's explore making a chalk stencil using a similar design.

stencil: *a method of producing images by cutting openings in a mask of plastic, metal, or other material so that pigment may go through the openings to the material beneath*

Printmaking Activities

2 On a strip of cardboard, draw the outlines of pueblos. Pueblos are Native American living places, or apartments. They have flat roofs and straight walls. Some are higher than others and some smaller. Draw completely across the cardboard.

3 Cut on the line of your drawing and separate the two pieces. These will be your stencils.

4 Place the cutout edge of one stencil about one-third of the way down a piece of paper and chalk the edge with blue chalk.

5 Holding the stencil firmly, brush the chalk up onto the paper with tissue.

6 Remove the stencil. You can see how the stencil created a blue sky and the outline of the pueblos.

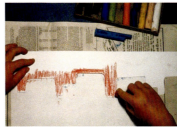

7 Now, place the other stencil over the chalked sky along the edge of the pueblos. Rub red, brown, or tan chalk on the edge of the stencil.

8 Hold the stencil firmly and brush the red chalk down onto the pueblos.

9 The stencil is removed and shows the soft color on the pueblos. Make other pueblo shapes the same way with different colors.

10 This is the completed stencil print. Doors and windows were added with chalk. With a stencil you can color certain areas of a print. Notice the values of colors. Can you see the light and dark values? Remember, value is the lightness and darkness of a color.

Art Activities with Paper, Clay, Fibers, and Printmaking: Using Masterworks as Inspiration

44 Nature Prints

Grade Level
4–8

Concept
Structure and texture of natural objects may be observed and printed.

Skill
Preparing and printing with natural materials; use of a brayer.

Resource
Student work

Materials
Fresh leaves and grasses that have been flattened and pressed overnight in newspapers under weights; newspapers; printing papers of various colors and textures; waterbased printing ink (colors as well as black); brayers; inking slabs. Optional: watercolors and brushes.

Procedure
Look at the example and analyze the process. If possible, use natural materials that the children can collect and press. Dry leaves will decompose in the printing process.

Organize the printing stations so that 5 or 6 children can move through each in one direction, past the leaves or grasses, brayer, inked slab and newspaper stack, printing paper, newsprint and clean brayer. It is useful to have each station monitored by a student who will replenish the printing ink as needed and make sure a clean printing area is made available for each student.

Children will brayer ink onto the back of one leaf at a time on newspaper, place it ink side up on a clean stack of newspaper, lay printing paper over it, and roll it with a clean brayer or press with fingertips. Older students may place the inked material ink side down on the printing paper, lay a clean newspaper on top, and roll with a clean brayer. This method is preferable if several leaves are to be printed and combined with watercolor. Let the prints dry completely before matting them.

This is a nature print made by the **relief** printing of different leaves. Remember that in relief printing the raised surface is inked and prints on paper. Gather green leaves of different shapes and sizes, and press them with books.

1 Now, prepare the paper on which your leaves will be glued. Brush clear water completely over a piece of watercolor paper.

2 Paint yellow and red watercolors on the wet paper. Let the colors blend together.

Printmaking Activities

3 Ink a brayer with a dark color ink and roll it over the back of the leaf.

4 Place the inked side of the leaf down on white paper. Then, roll a clean brayer over the leaf.

5 Remove the leaf from the paper. You can see the veins and shape of the leaf. Then, cut out the leaf. Print and cut out other prints of leaves.

7 Now, try making leaf prints directly on paper. Place a leaf on a piece of paper and roll the back with ink. Place the leaf inked side down on the printing paper. Place another piece of paper over it and roll it with a brayer. Print other leaves on the printing paper.

8 Here, you can see how a leaf acted as a stencil to make a print. This is the piece of paper on which a leaf was inked. The leaf blocked out the ink and an interesting print remained.

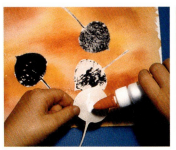 

6 Arrange the leaf prints in a random pattern, then glue them to the watercolor background.

relief: carving a surface in such a way that all that remains of the original surface is the design to be printed

9 This is a completed relief print made with leaves. Can you see the different kinds of leaves used to make this print?

93

45 Exploded Designs

Grade Level
5-8

Concept
A relief block can be made from cardboard to produce a collagraph print.

Skill
Making a low relief of cardboard and printing from it.

Resource
White is the Best Color by Glen Alps

Materials
Heavy cardboard 9 x 12 inches; lightweight shirt cardboard or tagboard 7 x 10 inches; printing paper; scissors; white glue; plastic spray; printing ink; brayers; inking slabs.

Procedure
Study the examples and explain that a collagraph is a relief print made by inking a collage made with materials that raise the surface of the printing plate. Note that the child's artwork is the result of cutting and expanding a single large shape.

Demonstrate how to cut a smaller cardboard in two, then separate the parts slightly on a larger cardboard. Cut one of the two pieces and separate these parts slightly. Continue to cut and separate the pieces until the "exploded" shapes are pushed apart to fill the entire area of the large cardboard. Let the children complete their designs to this point. Then, have them lift each piece of the design and glue it to the background support cardboard. Seal the design with plastic spray or by painting with diluted white glue. The children can then roll out printing ink with a brayer on the inking slab and ink the design, place a sheet of printing paper over it, and roll with a clean brayer or the bowl of a spoon.

Extension: Experiment with different kinds and colors of printing paper. Try mounting the printing plate alongside the best print made from it.

This is a **collagraph** called *White is the Best Color* by American artist Glen Alps. A collagraph is a relief print made by inking a collage made with materials that raise the surface of the printing plate.

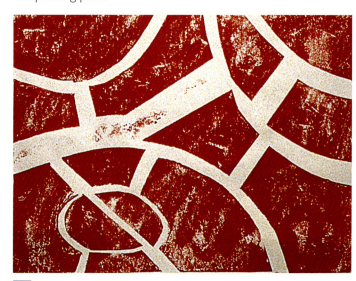

1 This is a completed exploded design. The plate for the print was made by gluing cutout shapes to a larger piece of cardboard.

2 You'll need one large piece of cardboard for the base of the plate and a smaller one for the relief printing surface.

collagraph: *a relief print made by inking a collage made with materials that raise the surface of the printing plate*

Printmaking Activities

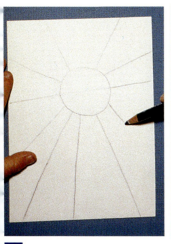

3 Draw a simple design of straight lines and curved lines. Cut out each shape created by the design.

4 Arrange the shapes on the larger piece of cardboard. Explode the design by pushing apart the shapes to fill the entire area.

5 Glue the shapes to the cardboard. The shapes are in relief or raised on the cardboard. This becomes your printing plate.

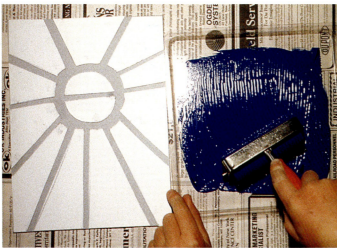

6 Now, roll a brayer with ink.

7 Roll the ink over the cardboard printing plate several times so the ink covers the raised surface. Place a piece of printing paper over it. Then, rub it all over with a spoon. Remove the paper from the plate. At left is the completed print.

8 Try making other abstract designs and use the exploded design technique to make a printing plate. This time, try painting or rolling different colors of ink on each shape.

9 This is the completed print with different colors.

Art Activities with Paper, Clay, Fibers, and Printmaking: Using Masterworks as Inspiration

46 Glue & String Prints

Grade Level
5-8

Concept
Glue and glued string both create linear designs that can be printed.

Skill
Creating a linear collagraph and printing from it.

Resource
Student work

Materials
Heavy cardboard about 5 x 7 inches or 6 x 9 inches; white glue in squeeze bottles; 3-5 yards of heavy string or twine, not yarn, for each student; plastic spray, polymer emulsion, or shellac and brushes; crayons; planning paper; printing paper; printing ink; brayers; inking slabs; scissors; craft sticks.

Procedure
Look at the example and review the concept that a collagraph is a built-up relief technique and that glue trailed onto cardboard alone or with string added will dry into a raised line that can be printed.

With crayons and planning paper, children will draw a linear design or picture composed of uncomplicated lines. The design is then drawn again on the heavy cardboard. Each line is traced with a smooth line of white glue. A few blobs, dots, and short lines can add texture to large shapes. Set the plate aside to dry overnight. Seal the design with plastic spray or polymer emulsion, diluted white glue, or shellac. (Be sure to wash brushes in thinner, if using shellac.) The children then roll printing ink out on the slab with a brayer and ink the glue design. They should not remove the ink that hits between the glue lines. They lay a sheet of printing paper on top, roll it with a clean brayer, and remove the print.

String prints can be made in the same manner by laying the string into the glue before it sets up, pushing it into place with a craft stick, and letting it dry. A few areas could be filled in solidly with string.

Glue and string can create a raised line design that can be printed. This is a print made by a student using this technique of relief printing. This kind of built-up relief is also called a collagraph.

1 We'll explore making a glue print first. Make a rough sketch of a design using only lines. Then, draw your subject again on heavy cardboard.

rubbing: *artwork created by placing paper over a relief surface and moving colored wax or other pigmented material over the paper until the image is delineated*

Printmaking Activities

2 Squeeze a line of glue over each line in your drawing.

6 Now, try making a glue and string print using a similar technique. Again, make a line drawing. Trace each line with glue. Place a line of string on the glue shaping it in place with a craft stick. The shapes can be filled in with glue and string, as you can see in the lower left and right pictures. After the glue has dried, ink the plate.

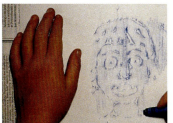

3 After the glue has dried, place a piece of paper over the cardboard plate, and rub the paper with a crayon. The raised glue lines will appear darker, and you will see the image. This is called a **rubbing**.

7 Place printing paper over the plate and rub it with a spoon.

4 Roll a brayer in ink, and roll it over the printing plate. Place your paper over the plate, and rub the paper with a spoon.

5 Remove the paper by starting at one end and pulling it off. This is the completed print. The inked glue lines created the image.

8 This is the completed print. Can you see how the raised relief made by the glue and string created this collagraph?

47 Multicolor Cardboard Printing

Grade Level
4-8

Concept
Cardboard relief prints can be multicolored.

Skill
Printing in register.

Resource
Mt. Fuji in Clear Weather by Katsushika Hokusai

Materials
Planning paper; heavy cardboard 6 x 9 inches; lightweight cardboard; scissors; white glue; plastic spray or polymer emulsion; black construction paper 9 x 12 inches; white, red, blue, and yellow printing ink; brayers, inking slabs; masking tape.

Procedure
Show Hokusai's woodblock print noting that it was printed in register with several colors.

Have students draw a design on planning paper of several large, simple shapes that do not touch one another. They transfer the design to light cardboard, cut out the shapes, and glue them in place on the heavy cardboard support. The surface is sealed with polymer emulsion or plastic spray. Then, they lay the plate on the table and outline the perimeter with masking tape to define its placement. A piece of printing paper is centered on top of it and outlined with more tape. When the paper and plate have been removed, the tape rectangles will indicate where they should be located to insure proper register in subsequent steps of the process.

Students roll white ink on the slab, ink the plate, and place it face-up in the smaller rectangle. (White adds luminosity to later colors.) Black paper is laid over it within the larger rectangle and rolled with a brayer. The students lift off the print, set it aside and continue to print other papers until the white ink is exhausted. On another slab, they roll red ink and apply the red to only one or two pieces of the design. The plate is replaced within the small rectangle, covered with the previously printed papers, and printed. Blue ink is applied on other parts of the plate and printed in the same way. Yellow ink is applied to the rest of the design and to some parts that earlier received red or blue ink and the papers are printed. Note the effects of printing multiple colors over white on the same plate.

Katsushika Hokusai, Japanese, 1760-1849. *Fuji in Clear Weather* (from the series *Thirty-six Views of Mt. Fuji*), early 1830s. Color woodblock print, 10 1/16 x 14 3/4 inches (25.60 x 37.50 cm). Cleveland Museum of Art, Bequest of Edward L. Whittemore, 1930.189.

This is a print by the Japanese artist Katsushika Hokusai (*Hoh*-koo-sigh). It was made by printing carved wood blocks. Each block was inked with a different color and printed in register. You can make a relief print with a similar technique.

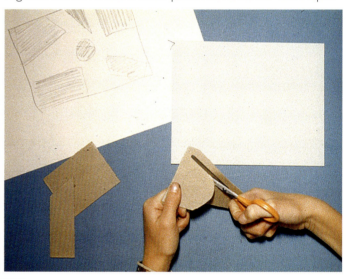

1 Draw a design of simple shapes, organic or geometric, on planning paper. Transfer the design to cardboard and cut out the shapes.

2 Arrange the shapes on heavy cardboard in your preplanned design. Glue the shapes to the cardboard. This will be your relief printing plate.

 Printmaking Activities

register marks: *the marks that are placed on the paper and the print plate to aid in lining up the paper in the printing process*

3 After coating the shapes with polymer emulsion, place the plate on a larger piece of paper, and outline the plate with tape. This will assure that the printing plate is always in the same place, or in register, when you are printing. Center a piece of printing paper on top of the plate, and outline it with tape. These **register marks** will assure that the printing paper is also in the same place each time it is printed with a different color.

4 Roll white ink on the brayer and ink the entire plate. The white ink adds luminosity to colors added later. Place the plate within the register marks, and place printing paper over it within its register marks. Rub the plate with a spoon.

5 Pull the print from the plate and set it aside. Continue printing on scrap paper until most of the ink is removed from the plate.

6 Now, apply red ink to some of the shapes, and print it on the printing paper, using the register marks.

7 Print yellow ink in the same way.

8 Then, print the final color blue and pull the print from the plate.

9 Here is the completed relief print. Notice how the white ink underneath the colors adds luminosity to them. The colors used for this relief print were primary colors, red, blue, and yellow, along with the neutral color, white.

99

Art Activities with Paper, Clay, Fibers, and Printmaking: Using Masterworks as Inspiration

48 Japanese Paint Prints

Grade Level
4-8

Concept
A multicolored paint print can simulate a Japanese woodblock print.

Skill
Designing and printing a simulated woodblock print.

Resource
Horse Mackerel and Prawn by Ando Hiroshige (hear-oh-*sheeg*-ay)

Materials
Planning paper; pencils; sheets of polyfoam or large styrofoam meat trays (without a logo) at least 4 x 6 inches; watercolor paints and small brushes; masking tape; smooth white drawing paper or rice paper.

Procedure
Look at Hiroshige's woodblock print and describe the process of Japanese woodblock printing where each color of the print is applied in a separate printing in register from many woodblocks that have been cut in register. Students will explore a much simplified version of this technique by preparing single blocks of polyfoam or styrofoam.

On planning paper, students will develop a design or picture wherein all the lines enclose shapes. This plan is transferred freely to the sheet of polyfoam and the lines retraced, pressing firmly to make grooves. Some areas should be textured, if desired, with stippling or crosshatching. Students cut a piece of printing paper 2 inches longer than the plate and tape it to the back so that it can be folded forward to cover the surface of the plate completely. With a small brush, they paint one section of the design with fairly thick watercolor. Immediately, while the paint is still wet, they bring the printing paper over it and press with the fingers or a spoon to transfer the color. Students continue to paint and print, paint and print, always keeping the paper taut as the design is transferred. A clean, white line should separate all of the areas of color. The polyfoam can be rinsed and dried and new colors can be painted on for another print.

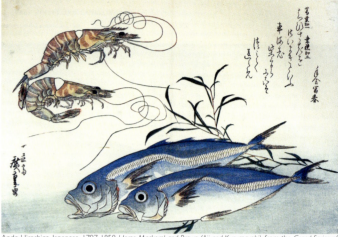

Ando Hiroshige, Japanese, 1797-1858. *Horse Mackerel and Prawn (Aji and Kurumayebi)*, from the *Grand Series of Fishes (Uwu-zukushi)*, c. 1832. Hand colored woodcut print, 13¾ x 9¾ inches (35 x 25 cm).

This is a print made by **woodblock printing**. We'll explore a simplified version of this technique by preparing a single block of styrofoam for printing.

woodblock print: *a relief print made by cutting a design into a block of wood and applying ink to the raised surface*

1 Develop a design where the lines enclose the shapes.

2 Prepare the plate by first cutting the edges from a styrofoam tray.

Printmaking Activities

3 Transfer the design to the styrofoam printing plate. Then retrace all the lines, pressing firmly to make grooves. Texture some of the areas by drawing lines or dots in the shapes.

4 Turn the plate over on a larger piece of printing paper. Fold one edge of the paper over the plate and tape it to the plate. This will keep the paper in register when it is printed.

5 Fold the paper to the side, and paint one section of the design with watercolor.

6 Fold the paper over the plate, and rub the painted area with a spoon.

7 Pull the print from the paper. You have printed one section of the design.

8 Follow the same steps to print the other colors. The last picture on the lower right shows the last color printed after it has been pulled from the plate. All of the colors are in register because the plate was taped to the printing paper.

9 The artist evaluates her completed print. She's checking the print to see if the colors are in register.

8 This is the completed relief print. A white line separates the shapes because the grooved lines were not inked. Can you see the texture in the leaves?

Art Activities with Paper, Clay, Fibers, and Printmaking: Using Masterworks as Inspiration

49 Chalk Monoprints

Grade Level
4-8

Concept
Indirect monoprinting may be combined with a chalk design for a mixed media print.

Skill
Combining chalk drawing with monoprinting.

Resource
Einstein on the Beach III by Red Grooms

Materials
White drawing paper; carbon paper; styrofoam meat trays or commerical polyfoam sheets; pencils and ballpoint pens; colored art chalk; brayers; inking slabs; waterbased black printing ink.

Procedure
Examine Grooms' monoprint and analyze how it was made. A monoprint is a single impression made from a master plate, block, or arrangement of objects.

Each student will cut the edges off a styrofoam tray to make a printing plate. On white paper, they will draw a rectangle a little smaller than the styrofoam and within it, draw a simple line design where lines enclose shapes. They place a piece of carbon paper carbon side up on the table, lay the paper over it, and redraw the design. With the carbon drawing facing up, students color in every shape with chalk using an interesting color scheme. Then, they roll out the ink on the slab with the brayer and cover the styrofoam with a thin, even coat. They place the chalk design gently facedown on the plate and carefully redraw every line with a ballpoint pen or a pencil with colored lead to be sure all of the lines are traced. Ask that they be careful not to touch the design with fingertips. They lift off the print. It should show fine, fuzzy black lines against chalked colors that have been set by the ink. The print can be matted to cover the outer edges.

Red Grooms, American, born 1937. *Einstein on the Beach III*, 1976. Monoprint. Courtesy Shark's Inc. © 2011 Red Grooms / Artists Rights Society (ARS), New York

This is a **monoprint** called *Einstein on the Beach III* by Red Grooms. A monoprint is a one-of-a-kind print. The artist draws the subject on a printing plate, lays paper on top of it, and prints it. You'll learn how indirect monoprinting is combined with a chalk design for a mixed media print.

1 Prepare a styrofoam tray to be used as a printing plate by cutting off the edges.

2 Draw a simple line design the same size as the styrofoam plate. Rows of houses with only windows and doors would be a good subject. Think of others that could be drawn where lines enclose the shapes.

Printmaking Activities

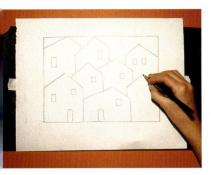

3 Place the design over a piece of carbon paper with the carbon facing up. Tape the carbon paper to your drawing. Then, trace all of the lines in your design.

4 Untape the paper from the carbon paper. The drawing has been transferred to the back of the paper.

5 With the carbon drawing facing up, color each shape with chalk.

6 Use bright, contrasting colors and fill all of the shapes.

7 Ink the entire plate with black ink.

8 Place the chalk design facedown on the plate, matching the edges of the chalk drawing with the edges of the plate.

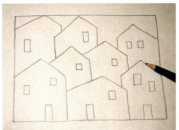

9 Redraw each line with a colored pencil to be sure all lines are traced. This will transfer ink to the print. Be careful not to touch the design area with your fingertips.

10 Now, pull the print from the plate. You can see where the ink has been transferred to the print.

11 Fuzzy black lines outline the colorful chalk shapes that have been set by the ink. The completed chalk monoprint can be matted and hung for display.

monoprint: *a one-off print created when paper is pressed down on a surface that has been decorated with printing ink or painted*

103

50 Textured Collagraphs

Grade Level
4–8

Concept
Textural prints can be made from textured collages.

Skill
Making a collagraph from a textural collage.

Resource
Growing Hill by Glen Alps

Materials
Collage materials of about the same thickness, such as heavy woven or knitted textiles, doilies, plastic berry baskets, toothpicks, embossed cardboard, thin sponge or cork, craft sticks, twine, washers; masonite or other rigid support; white glue or contact cement; scissors; printing ink; brayers; inking slab; printing paper; plastic spray.

Procedure
Look at Alps' collograph and discuss the process. Remind students of collages they have made with textured materials, recalling that a collage is a planned composition not just a collection of oddments. Suggest that they build their designs from several materials that are similar in thickness to make a very shallow relief.

Students will select, shape, and arrange textured materials to make a pleasing composition, repeating some textures and shapes for balance and interest. They glue the pieces down one at a time. Then the collage must be sealed by spraying it several times or painting it with shellac or polymer emulsion so that the porous materials will not absorb the ink. They ink the plate with the brayer. If white areas are desired in the print, they should either be wiped clean with a facial tissue or a shape of paper cut to mask them. The printing paper is placed over the plate and pressed with fingers or rubbed with the bowl of a spoon.

Glen Alps, American, 1914-1996. *Growing Hill.* Collagraph.

This **collagraph** by American artist Glen Alps is called *Growing Hill.* A collagraph is a print that is made from a textured collage. Textured materials like burlap, corrugated paper, and sandpaper can be inked and printed to make a collagraph.

1 Select scraps of textured material to make your collage. Burlap, sandpaper, and corrugated paper are all good materials.

2 Plan a design and cut shapes from the different textured materials. Repeat some textures and shapes for balance and interest.

collagraph: *a relief print made by inking a collage made with materials that raise the surface of the printing plate*

Printmaking Activities

3 Arrange the shapes on a large piece of cardboard.

4 Glue down the shapes. This will become your printing plate.

5 Here, students prepare their plates for printing by coating them with a spray or acrylic medium.

6 After the collage has been sealed, ink the plate with a brayer.

7 Place paper over the inked plate, and roll it with a brayer or rub it with a spoon.

8 Pull the print from the plate.

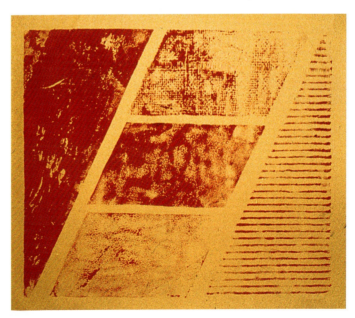

9 This is the completed collagraph. Notice the variety of textures and values that are created with these materials. Values are the lightness or darkness of a color. Can you identify them?

105

Art Activities with Paper, Clay, Fibers, and Printmaking: Using Masterworks as Inspiration

51 Acetate Intaglio

Grade Level
5-8

Concept
An intaglio print is made by transferring the ink in the scratches of a plate to paper.

Skill
Making a drypoint intaglio (in-*tahl*-ee-oh) print.

Resource
Self-Portrait by Rembrandt van Rijn

Materials
Planning paper; clear acetate or plexiglass; T-pins, large safety pins, or a drypoint needle; masking tape; tarlatan or old stockings; printing ink; brayers; ink slabs; printing paper, such as smooth watercolor paper; a sink or large tray; a wringer-type press with felts or blanket; a piece of thin masonite.

Procedure
Look at Rembrandt's drypoint print and describe the intaglio process as one where the print is made from ink left in the scratches after the surface has been carefully wiped off.

Students will make preliminary drawings on planning paper. They tape the drawing under a sheet of clear acetate and trace the lines with a drypoint needle or T-pin, scratching firmly but being careful not to cut through the plastic. They should vary the pressure for thick and thin lines and try cross-hatching. Have them run a finger over the surface and feel the "burr." Then, they ink the plate thoroughly making sure ink penetrates all of the cracks. With tarlatan or nylon, wadded up, they wipe the ink from the top surface. Wiping should leave ink only in the cracks. Have them give the plate a final wiping with the palm of the hand. Then the plate is placed on a piece of thin masonite and covered with a sheet of good quality paper that has been soaked in water for at least 30 minutes and blotted damp-dry. Over this "sandwich," carefully lay a thick felt or blanket, then feed it through the rollers of the press. Then the blanket/felt is removed and the print lifted from the plate.

Note: If a press is unavailable, rub the back of a spoon over the damp paper to transfer the ink. Check the print for problems before making another print. Problems may arise from too little scratching, too much or not enough ink, insufficient pressure, or paper that is too wet.

Rembrandt van Rijn, Dutch, 1606-1669. *Self-Portrait*, c. 1648; 1st state. Etching, retouched with drypoint. 6¼ x 5⅛ inches (16.1 x 13 cm). Photo: Gérard Blot. Louvre, Paris, France. Photo Credit: Réunion des Musées Nationaux / Art Resource, NY

This *Self-Portrait* by Rembrandt is a drypoint print. It was made by the **intaglio** method of printmaking. This is a technique which transfers ink to paper from lines etched, engraved, or scratched on the surface of a plate.

1 Plan the design for your drypoint print by drawing or painting it on paper. Here, a student has selected different kinds of brayers and a pencil as a subject.

2 Copy the design on tracing paper.

Printmaking Activities

3 Fasten the tracing paper under the clear plastic, then scratch in the design with a drypoint needle or T-pin.

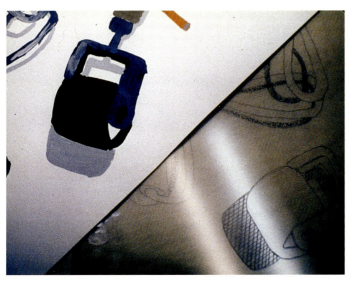

4 Scratch texture into your design by using crosshatching, and vary the pressure for thick and thin lines. Here, you can compare the original drawing with the drypoint plate.

6 Then, wipe the ink off the surface of the plastic with a paper towel wrapped around a block. The ink should remain only in the scratched lines.

7 Put the plastic plate on a printing press and cover it with dampened printing paper and several pieces of blanket, or felts. Run the plate, paper, and felts through the press. Remove the felts, and pull the print from the plate.

5 After the plate is completed, rub ink onto the surface.

intaglio: printmaking technique which transfers ink to paper from areas etched, engraved, or scratched beneath the suface of a plate

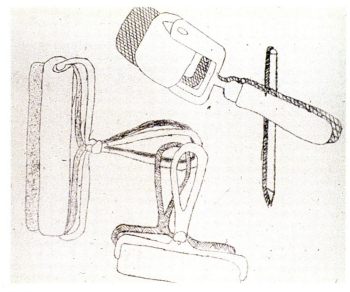

8 This is the completed drypoint print. Only the areas that were scratched in the plastic plate printed on the paper. Can you see the shaded areas that were crosshatched? This gives a three-dimensional effect.

Art Activities with Paper, Clay, Fibers, and Printmaking: Using Masterworks as Inspiration

52 Corrugated Collagraphs

Grade Level
5-8

Concept
A corrugated relief print uses textures to create light, middle, and dark values.

Skill
Creating a print in three values.

Resource
The White Square by Glen Alps

Materials
Pieces of corrugated box cardboard; newsprint; printing paper; printing ink; plastic spray, polymer emulsion, or diluted white glue; pencils; inking slab; X-acto knives or single-edged razor blades; tweezers; brayers; newspapers.

Procedure
Look at the example and remind students that a collagraph is a relief print made by inking a collage made with materials that raise the surface of the printing plate. Review the concept of value, gradations from light to dark, and explain that this printing experience shows dark values from solid printed areas, middle values from striped printed areas, and light values from imprinted areas.

On newsprint, students plan designs that incorporate three values. Important: Plan to leave the shapes around the outside solid, to avoid breaking down the edges of the plate. Have them plan large, simple shapes. They should test the corrugated cardboard to find on which side the paper "skin" can be most easily removed. They transfer the design to this side. Then, they cut around all of the areas that are to remain light and remove both the top paper and the corrugated parts, or they could cut through the cardboard entirely. They cut around the areas that will show the middle value and remove only the top paper layer. Tweezers can be used to lift out tiny pieces. A damp sponge can be used to moisten the surface and make it easier to peel off. The plate is sprayed with plastic sealer, or use polymer emusion or diluted white glue before inking and printing the plate.

Extensions: Tear off some of the paper skin to leave irregular shapes; pierce the solid areas with a compass point to create another texture.

Glen Alps, American, 1914-1996. *The White Square.* Collagraph.

This is a **collagraph** called *The White Square* by American artist Glen Alps. Remember, a collagraph is a relief print made by inking a collage made with materials that raise the surface of the printing plate.

1 This is a collagraph plate and print. The plate was made by removing the paper from the top of a corrugated cardboard, cutting some areas completely away, and leaving the cardboard surface on others. This created light, medium, and dark values in the collagraph.

collagraph: *a relief print made by inking a collage made with materials that raise the surface of the printing plate*

Printmaking Activities

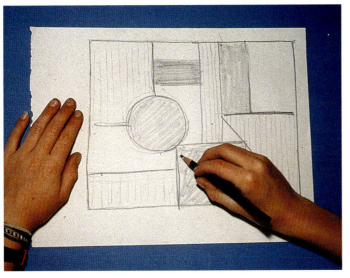

6 Roll the brayer in the ink until the roller is completely covered.

7 Then, ink the entire plate making sure that all relief surfaces are inked.

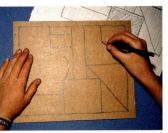

2 To make a corrugated collagraph, first draw a design of geometric shapes, and add values to the shapes.

3 Draw the design again on a piece of corrugated cardboard.

8 Place a piece of printing paper over the plate.

9 Then, pull the print from the plate. You can see that no ink prints where the shapes were removed.

4 Score the lines around the shapes where you want a medium value. Then, peel away as much paper as you can.

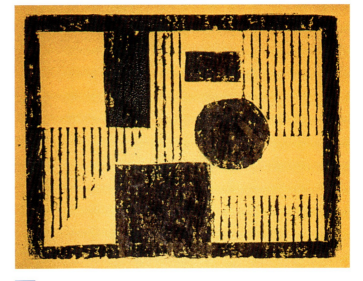

5 To completely expose the corrugated areas, moisten them with water, then the paper is easily removed. Be sure all the shapes are removed from the areas where you want a light value. The shapes to have dark values remain untouched.

10 This is the completed collagraph. The solid shapes created dark values. Where the corrugated was exposed, medium values were created. Light values on the print show where the corrugated was completely away. Can you see these values?

109

53 Linoleum Prints

Grade Level
5–8

Concept
Linoleum can be used to make relief prints.

Skill
Making a linoleum block print.

Resource
Still Life Under a Lamp by Pablo Picasso (*pah*-blow pee-*kahs*-oh)

Materials
Linoleum; V and U gouges, at least two sizes; tracing paper; newsprint; soft lead pencils, pens, India ink; printing paper, such as Japanese rice paper; printing ink; brayer; inking slab; newspapers. Optional: a printing press.

Procedure
Look at Picasso's print and see how the linoleum was cut and the different colors were printed. Multicolor linoleum prints are made by preparing and printing a separate block for each color in subsequent "runs." Students will work with only one block in this lesson. Pre-mounted linoleum on ¾-inch thick plywood blocks is available. Linoleum cuts best at room temperature or warmer.

Each student will select one from several preliminary sketches and draw it more precisely with a soft lead pencil on the linoleum surface. Students should remember that the image will print reversed. They place the drawing face down on the linoleum and rub it firmly to transfer the pencil drawing. Using a sharp V gouge, they cut a narrow groove outside the edge of every black area to establish the outline. Remember to keep the plate-holding hand always behind the cutting tool, in case of a slip. Using different sizes and shapes of gouges, students remove the linoleum from areas that are not to receive any ink. They should use the gouges selectively to produce interesting lines and textures within the black shapes. They should leave some parts of the background uncut for a more lively treatment. Then, they roll a minimum of ink onto the plate and make a "proof" print using a printer's press or by rolling a baren or the back of a spoon over the back of the paper. When experimentation produces the correct blend of inking and pressure, they can make a "run" of several prints. They should sign and number them as a professional artist does.

Pablo Picasso, Spanish, 1881–1973. *Still Life with Glass Under the Lamp (Nature morte au verre sous la lampe)*, 1962. Linoleum cut, plate: 20⅞ × 25³⁄₁₆ inches (53 × 64 cm); sheet: 24½ × 29⅝ inches (62 × 75.2 cm). Gift of Mrs. Donald B. Straus. Digital Image © The Museum of Modern Art/Licensed by SCALA / Art Resource, NY © 2011 Estate of Pablo Picasso / Artists Rights Society (ARS), New York

This is a linoleum print called *Still Life Under a Lamp* by Spanish artist Pablo Picasso. It was printed by printing separate blocks of linoleum for each color. Notice how sharp and crisp the edges of each color are. We will see how a single linoleum block is used for relief printing in this activity.

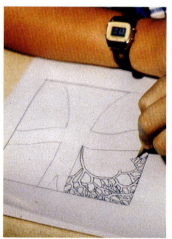 

1 Draw a design with pencil on tracing paper the size of the linoleum block you will be printing. Turn the drawing over on the linoleum block and rub it so that the image is transferred.

2 You can see the transferred image here.

Printmaking Activities

6 Now, pull the print from the plate. You can see that the carved areas do not print.

3 Now, carve out the areas that are not to be printed. Warming the linoleum block with an iron will make the carving easier.

4 Using a brayer, ink the plate.

7 This student has pulled several prints from the linoleum block plate. Additional colors may be printed, but a separate linoleum block must be prepared for each color.

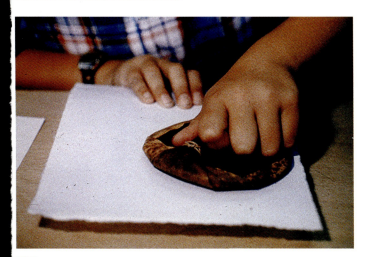

5 Place printing paper over the inked block and rub with a **baren**. The baren applies even pressure when printing relief prints.

baren: *circular flat pad used to press the print down on the block during woodblock or linoleum printing*

8 This is the completed print of a tree. The cutout areas on the linoleum block did not print creating the interesting textured design. Can you see the areas that were carved in the linoleum plate and those that were not?

Drawing and Painting Activities: Using Masterworks as Inspiration

abstract: art which depicts subject matter with simplified or symbolic forms. Subject matter may be recognizable or may be completely transformed into shapes, colors, and/or lines.

accordion fold: zigzag fold in which a sheet of paper has two or more parallel folds that open in the manner of an accordion.

Adinkra: symbols, originally created in west Africa, that represent concepts or motifs. Used on fabric, pottery, woodcarvings, and logos.

armature: a framework on which a sculpture is molded with clay or similar material

atmospheric perspective: method of creating an illusion of distance in a work of art by depicting objects that are farther away in diminished colors and with less clarity of detail.

banner: a long strip of cloth bearing a slogan or design, hung in a public place or carried in a procession.

baren: circular flat pad used to press the print down on the block during woodblock or linoleum printing

batik: a process used to add color and design to paper or cloth; wax is the material utilized to protect areas from coloration by the dyes.

brayer: a hand roller used in printmaking techniques to spread ink or to offset an image from a plate to paper.

center of interest: a visual focal point of a work of art toward which all visual movement is directed.

collage: art technique in which materials such as paper, cloth, or found objects are glued to a backing.

collagraph: a relief print made by inking a collage made with materials that raise the surface of the printing plate

composition: the planned arrangement and organization of the elements of design in a work of art.

cool colors: hues in the purple to green range on the color wheel.

crosshatching: a method of creating value by drawing sets of parallel lines that intersect with one another.

geometric shapes: shapes with perfect, uniform measurements that don't often appear in nature

gesture drawing: fluid, continuous line drawings made quickly to show a subject that has motion.

graphic design: a creative process which combines words, symbols, and images to create a visual representation of ideas and messages.

haiku: a Japanese poem of seventeen syllables, in three lines of five, seven, and five, traditionally evoking images of the natural world

hand puppet: a puppet with a cloth body and hollow head that fits over the hand.

hatching: creating value by drawing parallel lines

helmet mask: a mask that is worn over the top of the head like a helmet for rituals, celebrations, and protection.

Huichol: indigenous people of west central Mexico, living in the Sierra Madres Occidental range in the Mexican states of Nayarit, Jalisco, Zacatecas, and Durango.

intaglio: printmaking technique which transfers ink to paper from areas etched, engraved, or scratched beneath the surface of a plate

kiln: a very hot oven used to bake and harden materials such as clay and bricks.

landscape: a work of art that uses natural scenery as subject matter.

mannequin: a framework with movable parts used to show the proportion of body parts or for drawing the body from different angles.

mask: a covering for all or part of the face, used for protection or decoration.

mobile: a group of hanging objects that move freely.

model: representation of a proposed structure to communicate design ideas to clients and the public

mola: a textile made by sewing layers of colored cloth together to form patterns.

monoprint: a one-off print created when paper is pressed down on a surface that has been decorated with printing ink or painted

mosaic: art consisting of a design made of small pieces of colored stone or glass

Navajo: the second largest Native American tribe of the United States of America.

organic shapes: shapes with a natural look and a flowing and curving appearance.

origami: the Japanese art of folding paper into decorative shapes and figures.

piñata: decorated container filled with toys and candy; suspended for blindfolded children to break with sticks.

portrait: a painting of a person that gives an impression of his or her character and appearance.

primary colors: three main colors (red, yellow, and blue) that can be combined to make all other colors.

relief: carving a printing surface in such a way that all that remains of the original surface is the design to be printed.

register marks: the marks that are placed on the paper and the print plate to aid in lining up the paper in the printing process

rubbing: artwork created by placing paper over a relief surface and moving colored wax or other pigmented material over the paper until the image is delineated.

sculpture: three-dimensional piece of art that has been modeled, cast, carved, or constructed.

secondary colors: colors that contain equal amounts of the two primary colors adjacent to them on the color wheel. Violet, green, and orange are the secondary colors.

self-portrait: a portrait of the artist made by him- or herself.

stabile: a freestanding abstract sculpture, typically of wire or sheet metal, in the style of a mobile but rigid and stationary.

stencil: a method of producing images by cutting openings in a mask of plastic, metal, or other material so that pigment may go through the openings to the material beneath.

symmetry: a balanced proportion of parts arranged on opposite sides of a plane, a line, or a point. The opposite of symmetry is asymmetry.

three-dimensional: having height, length, and width, as, for example, a sculpture.

two-dimensional: having length and height, as, for example, a painting.

warm colors: hues in the red to yellow range of the spectrum or color wheel.

warp: the set of lengthwise yarns through which the weft is woven.

weft: the horizontal threads that are interlaced through the warp in a woven fabric.

woodblock print: a relief print made by cutting a design into the flat surface of a block of wood and applying ink to the raised surface.

wycinanki: the art of Polish papercutting.

Elements and Principles of Design

Design refers to the plan or organization of an object in the environment — the arrangement of independent parts to form a coordinated whole. Design is achieved through the use of elements and principles.

Elements of Design are the content of most art activities: they include color, line, value, texture, shape, form, and space. The elements of design are the raw materials of an artist – the visual components of art.

a. **Color:** Color depends on light because it is made of light. There must be light for us to see color. Hue, value, and intensity are the three main characteristics of color.

b. **Line:** Line is a mark made by a pointed tool — brush, pencil, pen, etc. — and is often defined as a moving dot. It can vary in width, direction, curvature, length, and even color. Line often suggests movement in a work of art.

c. **Value:** Value refers to dark and light; the value scale refers to black and white with all gradations of gray in between. Value contrasts help us to understand a two-dimensional work of art.

d. **Texture:** Texture refers to the surface quality, both simulated and actual, of artwork. Using a dry brush technique creates simulated texture while heavy application of paint produces actual texture.

e. **Shape:** Shape is an area that is contained within an implied line, or is seen because of color or value changes. Shapes have two dimensions, length and width, and can be geometric or freeform.

f. **Form:** Shape and form have the same qualities but shape is two-dimensional and form is three-dimensional; it describes volume and mass. Both may be freeform or geometric, natural or man-made.

g. **Space:** Actual space is a three-dimensional volume that has width, height, and depth. Space in a painting is an illusion that creates a feeling of depth. Paintings are divided into positive space (the object itself) and negative space (the surrounding area).

Principles of Design refer to the way that the elements are arranged in a unified whole. The principles help to coordinate the elements for effective visual results.

a. **Unity:** Visual unity is one of the most important aspects of well-designed art. Unity provides the cohesive quality that makes a work feel complete.

b. **Balance:** Balance refers to the distribution of visual weight in a work of art. Balance can be either symmetrical or asymmetrical.

c. **Contrast:** Contrast refers to differences in values, colors, textures, shapes, and other elements. Contrast creates visual excitement and adds interest to the work. If all the elements — value, for example — are the same, the result is monotonous and unexciting.

d. **Movement:** Movement directs viewers through a work, often to a focal area. Movement can be directed along lines, edges, shapes, and colors, but moves the eye most easily on paths of equal value.

e. **Rhythm:** Rhythm is the repetition of visual movement — colors, shapes, or lines. Movement and rhythm work together to create the visual equivalent of a musical beat.

f. **Emphasis:** Emphasis creates dominance and focus. Artists can emphasize color, value, shapes, or other art elements to achieve dominance. Contrast can be used to emphasize a center of interest.

g. **Pattern:** Pattern uses elements in planned or random repetitions in a work of art. Pattern increases visual excitement by enriching surface interest.